# Evangelism in the Established Church

## By Jason L Kortering

Published by the evangelism committee of
First Protestant Reformed Church:
2800 Michigan Street NE, Grand Rapids, MI 49596

# Foreword

Evangelism work in the local congregation has everything to do with the gospel. It is the message of salvation which Christ has instructed the church to bring to all nations. The beginning place for this great activity is in the established church. Every Lord's Day the pastor is called by God to sound forth its message from the pulpit. The people are called to embrace Christ Jesus by faith and to live holy lives of thankfulness. Included in this response of faith is that the members of the congregation take this gospel and speak of it to others. Parents are to do this within covenant homes. Christian school teachers have the privilege to take the gospel and work out its implication in the class room. Laboring people take this same gospel and both by word and deed glorify God as Christians in the midst of a wicked world. As citizens of our country and as neighbors to others, we all have the privilege to take this same gospel and be ready to tell others why we are Christians and how they too may enjoy the same privileges of faith. All such activity is included in the prophetic office we possess as believers.

The message needs to be sounded forth. Every one of our churches will prosper in their outreach ministry through their Church Extension Committees or Evangelism Committees if we put into practice the exercise of personal witnessing. It is the necessary and wonderful link which joins committee activity with every member of the congregation. Only in this way, the entire church will be joined together in the important work of evangelism. We will be a mission church in the real sense of the Word.

Even then, we must always be reminded that evangelism is God's work. True, He uses human means and it is this fact that challenges every reader to address this work with humility and prayer before God. Only the Son of God gathers His church by His Word and Spirit. Obedience to that Word and humbly seeking His Holy Spirit to bless us assures us that this labor is not in vain in the Lord.

I want to thank the Evangelism Committee of the First Protestant Reformed Church in Grand Rapids, Michigan, for seeing this need, their willingness to take up this project, and all the work that brings it into print. May God bless these efforts to His glory.

Pastor J. Kortering

# INDEX

# Introduction

Most, if not all, of our congregations have an "Evangelism Committee" or have what is sometimes called a "Church Extension Committee." The general purpose of such a committee is to put forth effort to get the message of the gospel, as proclaimed in the local church and in our churches, to those who are without. The scope of their labors usually is not limited by geographic proximity to the local congregation; rather, most of them develop contacts anywhere in the world. The reason for this is obvious: whenever efforts are put forth to get the Word out into the world, God is sovereign in its distribution. An interested person who lives next door to the church building may send a copy of some literature to a member of their family who lives in Brazil, and one never knows where all of this may lead. Truth is that most of the effort of our evangelism committees is concentrated in our own local area. This is good and proper, for the purpose of all such effort is to be obedient to the mission mandate to begin at Jerusalem and then go unto the uttermost parts of the world. We begin our outreach with those who are closest to us and then extend the contact to others.

These committees have to be commended for their efforts to diversify the approach. Let me just list a few of those efforts. They publish and distribute literature; some of them even develop a rather extensive mailing list. Closely connected to this is a tape ministry. They prepare and distribute both audio and video copies of messages on various subjects. In some instances, this has led to the broadcast of the worship service over both radio and cable television. Others make use of our denominational broadcast and sponsor that in the local area. Usually, the committees sponsor some form of seminar or lecture series on a current subject of interest and advertise that so others can attend. On a more intimate level, some committees become involved in Bible Studies that are geared to a specific audience; it may be college students or anyone interested in the study of a certain subject. Another method used is "Newspaper Evangelism," in which a certain brief message is published in the local paper with a view to the general public reading it and becoming acquainted with some important aspect of truth. At various times effort is put forth to contact the neighbors. This can be done through mailings or by personal distribution as the members go door to door. The emphasis here is to acquaint the neighbors with the gospel or with some aspect of its message, which may include a special invitation to come and worship or to attend some specific event. Finally, there are more specific ministries to meet special needs that may include prison ministries, hospital visitations, and such like. If my memory is correct, I think that some of our pastors have in the past engaged in "street preaching." That may be more European or Asian, so I am sure many of our foreign readers are familiar with this ministry as well.

The effectiveness of all such outreach efforts is connected with personal contact. This is true because the goal of outreach is to communicate the gospel. The chief means to that end is the preaching of the gospel. The real encounter of all ministries is that one may come to hear the voice of our Lord Jesus Christ Himself. It stands to reason, then, that the efforts of outreach by the Evangelism Committee must be personal. Yes, God may use a piece of literature sent through the mail, but nothing can compare to that same piece of literature given by one person to another. It allows for more opportunity not only to talk, but far more importantly, to convey the love of Christ, which is what the gospel is all about. Methods that involve face-to-face contact are far more effective for this same reason. God uses human instrumentality to convey to others the sincerity of the message. Urgency, conviction, passion, and love are demonstrated in personal contact.

The conclusion that I draw from this is twofold. The first is that our membership must be personally involved in the efforts of the Church Extension Committee if these efforts are to be effective. Every one of us as members of the congregation must know what our committee is doing and we must ask ourselves, how can I do my part to make that effort more effective? A committee trying to do outreach without the involvement of the members is greatly handicapped. Secondly, the motivation to do this rests in the fundamental calling of every member to be burdened with the spiritual welfare of his neighbor. The heartbeat of all evangelism in the local church is the living testimony of a godly walk by the members and their eagerness to share the gospel with those who cross their pathway. The great motivation for effective evangelism in the local church is a heart that truly loves God and loves the neighbor for God's sake. If we truly love God, the goal of evangelism is not self, not even the neighbor, but it is God and His glory through the gathering and strengthening of His precious people.

The purpose of this book (originally published as a short series of articles in the *Standard Bearer*) is to motivate each member of the local church to be personally active in evangelism and to give the work of the Evangelism Committee the spiritual impetus it needs.

One approach I like to take is to encourage you to read some of the challenging literature on this subject. More than likely we need help if we are to reach out personally to our neighbor. Interestingly, we have very few Protestant Reformed publications from which we can quote. Precious little has been written on the subject of missions and local evangelism. Our Evangelism Committees have observed that we have very little literature specifically written for non-Christians. We do not have booklets that guide the committees in various methods of personal outreach. We cannot pick up a Protestant Reformed publication that helps our members share their personal faith with a non-Christian. I am not being critical here, nor am I belittling our past efforts, for I understand very well our history and the focus of our attention.

We must not reason, however, that since we did not have need for such material in the past, we do not need it today. Certainly, I trust our discerning readers will understand that the great blessing of God upon our churches and their history is that now is the time for outreach. We have been guided by God's providential history to clearly set forth the Reformed faith, especially as it relates to the gospel and its preaching. In addition to that, we have been tested in our sincerity of that faith by a massive split in our churches. God has enabled us to recover; we have gone from strength to strength, as is evidenced in the practical demonstration of love for our children in covenant instruction. These events have taken the lion share of our efforts and they have been greatly blessed by God, so that now we stand strong in the truth of the gospel and the covenant and in the practical working out of these convictions in our daily life. Now is the time that we can truly say, from this foundation of strength, God commands us to reach out and share this with others.

I am convinced there is no church that has the gospel of the "full counsel of God" as we do. We have consistently worked out the practical implications of the antithesis in our daily life. God does not want us to keep this simply for ourselves; it is this glorious truth that God has committed to us to share with others, even at this late date in history. As we reach outside our churches, we will accomplish two things: we will witness to non-Christians and bring the gospel to them, and we will encourage fellow saints outside our churches. Probably more than at any other time in history, our fellow saints need encouragement to stand for the truth, even unto death. We need to show God's love to our neighbors, whether they are here in America or young Christians in remote countries throughout the world. True unity and love is critical in these last days, and we as Christians must put forth effort to do our part.

Besides this, there is one more reason why it is necessary that we emphasize personal contact with our neighbor. Our social culture has changed. We have shifted from a predominantly agricultural society to a highly urbanized one through economic changes. As a result of this, personal contact with our neighbors has diminished. I remember the day when members of the rural community died, the local church bell would toll the number of his/her years. It was a moving tribute to everyone who lived in the town and adjacent country. Now we cannot even have a procession to the cemetery because drivers rudely interrupt the cars of the procession. With automatic garage door openers we come and go without even seeing our neighbors. Emphasis on privacy laws make us afraid as to how much we can even talk about our faith with others when we do have a face-to-face chat. If there was ever a time when we needed encouragement and instruction how to share our faith with our neighbors it is now. That is why we need to face this as we have not done before.

Having said this, I must admit that it is not easy to recommend what books can be helpful. If our attitude is that we have to be completely in agreement with a book or it cannot be read or used, we are in desperate straits, for there are precious few such books on outreach. I like to believe that our readers are mature enough to read with discernment, as we must with almost all books. The ultimate test of any writing must always be the Word of God. Preferred writers are those who set forth their ideas from a Reformed perspective. Even then, we must be discerning. Others may be able to give us suggestions, especially in some of the practical ways of interacting with non-Christian neighbors. They too must be tested by the Word of God.

One book that I found encouraging is entitled *Get Out* by G. VanDooren. This book is out of print and can be found only in libraries. Since it was written in 1972 when immigrants from the Netherlands had settled in Canada, the author addresses the attitude of the people in which they express their fear to share the gospel with others. Much of this is evident in our churches today as well. Let me quote from the introduction:

> The general single topic of the following pages will be to underline the necessity for the Church of Jesus Christ to "become an open Church."
>
> "Being" and "becoming" always go together in the Scriptures. Paul, addressing the "saints" in his letters, does not get tired of pointing out that they have to become, more and more, in daily conversation and sanctification, what they already are "in Jesus Christ."
>
> Being the true Church must never mean that we have attained it and now can relax. When the Heidelberg Catechism speaks (L.D. 44) of "a small beginning of the new obedience," this should not only be understood as applying to the individual believer, but also to the community and fellowship of the believers.
>
> By the expression, "an open Church" we do not only stress that according to our nature, the Church of Jesus Christ welcomes every one who desires to join her in true faith but also that she looks around, opens her arms, "goes out" to bring in the lost, in one word, the Church bears the image of her Savior, Jesus Christ."

Will Metzger wrote *Tell the Truth*. This book is still in print and published by InterVarsity Fellowship. It is the one I used when we had a special class on outreach when I pastored our Grandville PRC. It has Reformed emphasis, contrasts the man-centered gospel with the God-centered one. It is not simply a book on principles, but it has many practical suggestions on how to do outreach in the local church and in your personal life.

*Going and Growing* is a book written by Dick and Thea VanHalsema when they were involved in Reformed Bible College. They brought the Baker Mission Lecture series to that school in 1990 and these are summaries of their messages. I don't know if it is available today. Let me quote from this book,

> In the spring of 1983, Robertson McQuilkin, president of Columbia Bible College, visited RBC in Grand Rapids, Michigan to present the twelfth annual series of Baker Mission Lectures.
>
> From a lifelong involvement in missions—including twelve years of missionary service in Japan—President McQuilkin asked why Christ's Great Commission captures the enthusiasm and enlists the service of so few Christians.
>
> The speaker stated his own conclusions about why mission laborers are in such short supply. McQuilkin ventured to say that, in general, Christians have "heart trouble" (Christians do not love, do not really care about those who are outside of Christ). We have "eye trouble" (we do not see the plentiful harvest on the one hand and the shortage of workers on the other). We have "head trouble" (that something is wrong with our thinking processes, our brains, when we spend most of our time in theological speculation instead of engaging in witness and evangelization). Again, the guest speaker charged that Christians are prone to have "knee trouble" (for many, prayer is a neglected means of grace) and "ear trouble" (God calls, but we do not listen or obey).
>
> President McQuilkin's main point was that many Christians have exchanged the "Great Commission" for the "Great Omission."

We must also mention a couple of the classics: *God–Centered Evangelism*, by R. B. Kuiper; *Evangelism and the Sovereignty of God*, by J. I. Packer. Even though Charles

7

Haddon Spurgeon was addressing pastors when he gave the lectures contained in *The Soul Winner,* and though he comes from a believers' baptism tradition, he still inspires me as only Spurgeon can. He was a Calvinist who had a burden for lost souls. I am sure he will inspire you as well.

# 1. The Role of Every Believer in Evangelism

In the introduction we have set forth that the work of evangelism in the local church must involve every member of the congregation. No matter what project is undertaken, be it door-to-door evangelism, radio ministry, sponsoring local lectures, or whatever, it requires the active involvement of every member to accomplish its stated goal. Now we will develop a bit more why this is not only necessary, but also proper, and why it is to be expected by those who are working hard in this evangelism.

I address this question to every reader: Are YOU actively involved in outreach yourself and not just passing this work off to your pastor, the Evangelism Committee in your local church, or even to other members? The burden of this article is to show from the Bible that God has saved YOU to evangelize and that the leaders of the church want YOU to be busy in evangelism and expect it of YOU. This is God's way.

John Sittema, in an article in the Outlook of October 2003, raised the question why it is that in the past both Presbyterian and Reformed churches were zealous in outreach and missions, but now seem to have lost the passion for the lost. He writes,

> Local evangelism is almost nonexistent. Sadly a correlative attitude seems to be acceptable and popular among Calvinists these days: people get saved in Baptist or other fundamentalistic churches and then they learn good theology and become Calvinists. If it weren't so arrogant, it might be funny. Fact is that not many 'get saved' through evangelism effort of Calvinistic churches in todays Christian world. And that's a shame.

9

If we are honest with ourselves, we must admit that we fall under this criticism as well. We can say so easily that the church is being gathered from all nations under heaven and when that is complete, and we are very close to that completion, Christ will return. Do we realize what little effort is being put forth from Reformed churches, including ourselves, to do this work? Just consider India as an example and discover how little effort is put forth among those billion plus people. It is so small, it hardly seems to count. The same is true for Africa, including Ghana. I ask you, are we really doing all we can as churches in our mission work? We are doing something in mission work, and we in no way want to belittle that; it is cause for thanksgiving to God. Could we do more? If you really believe we could do more, then I also ask, why are we not doing it?

Mission zeal has something to do with it. I ask myself, what does it take to generate more zeal for missionary work and evangelism among our members? This ought to be the burden of every member of our churches. It is not honest simply to say, "We have zeal." It is not enough to say, "To generate zeal is the concern of consistories in the local church." Yes, they have their responsibility to promote missions. I am convinced that the real issue is spiritual and lies in the heart of every one of us. Every member must accept it as his calling to evangelize, and when we get this straight, we will discover under God's blessing that our churches will become truly more mission minded. I share the burden which G. VanDooren expressed for his churches in the book *Get Out*,

> Better a local congregation with no evangelistic organization whatsoever but fully alive "in the Lord," than a place with much noise of committees and sub-committees and all the works, but no life of the Spirit and no love for the neighbor.

God emphasizes that every saved person must speak of the wonderful works of God to everyone! A converted soul has within him a burning desire to praise and extol the name of the God who saved him. This is obviously true for new converts in the mission field, but it ought to be just as true for one saved within God's covenant. The Bible says in I Peter 2:4-10,

> Ye also as lively stones are built up a spiritual house, an holy priesthood, to offer up spiritual sacrifices, acceptable to God by Jesus Christ.... Ye are a chosen generation, a royal priesthood, an holy nation, a peculiar people; that ye should shew forth the praises of him who hath called you out of darkness into his marvelous light.

The word "to shew forth" is "to declare, to make known" the praises, virtues, and wonders of God. This is not limited to ministers, elders, and deacons; it is the task of every stone in the living house of God. The purpose of our salvation is to declare to everyone who crosses our pathway, our neighbor, that God is sovereign, He is great and greatly to be praised.

This is so rudimentary that I need not belabor the point. The shepherds led the way, for after having beheld by faith the wonder of the incarnation, they rejoiced in their salvation, and declared the message of the gospel to all. "When they had seen it, they made known abroad the saying which was told them concerning this child. And all they that heard it wondered at those things which were told them by the shepherds" (Luke 2:17, 18). This is the irrepressible joy of heart that motivates every Christian to share the gospel with his neighbor. He cannot but speak to his precious covenant child at home. No less can he be silent before the coarse sinner with whom he works on the job.

The motive is obvious; it is love, pure love. Jesus illustrated this with His reference to the forgiven debtors in

Luke 7:40-50. Why did the forgiven debtor find it easy to forgive his debtors? Jesus put it this way: when one is forgiven a great debt, he finds it easy to forgive someone who owes him a little. In the narrative, Jesus mentioned how Simon criticized Jesus' evangelistic work with the local prostitute because he did not know his own forgiveness of sins. If we truly know the horror of our sins and the depth of God's love to wash them away in the blood of Jesus, relief and joy motivate us to want others to enjoy this. The mark of a true Christian convert is his eagerness to see others saved even as he is saved.

It is the task of the ministry of the gospel and the teaching ministry of the local church to promote this activity in every member. I agree with VanDooren when he writes in *Get Out*,

> Assuming that consistories have to "appoint" committees, let them never instruct those committees, "to promote evangelism among the membership." That should never be the task of a committee which is only to give a helping hand to "God's own people," the "promotion" has to be done by the officebearers themselves, who have to equip the saints for the work of ministry, and are not allowed to "delegate" this Christ-given mandate to others. (cf Eph 4:11ff)

Every pastor has the commission from Christ so to conduct himself in his ministry and by example that he motivates every member to evangelize. In this way the congregation understands this to be their duty and that they ought to exercise it faithfully to the glory of God. Such instruction is part of the gospel, written in the Holy Bible. If we preach the whole counsel of God, it will include instruction in this labor.

The reference VanDooren makes is to Ephesians 4:11-14. There Paul instructs the Ephesian church leaders concerning their work. "And he gave some apostles, and some prophets, and some evangelists; and some pastors and teachers for the perfecting of the saints, for the work of ministry, for the edifying of the body of Christ." We have a misplaced comma here. It ought to read that the work of pastors and teachers is for the perfecting of the saints for the work of ministry. The ministry (service to others) is that done by the saints. The pastors and elders have the commission to equip the members so that they mature (perfecting) and are thus qualified to be active in service, ministry, which in turn edifies the body of Christ. This ministry includes attending to the needs of fellow members, assisting in training children of the covenant, helping the poor in the midst of the congregation, visiting the lonely, and doing the work of evangelism by sharing the gospel with others and thereby bringing others into the fellowship of the congregation.

In summary we say, when God works salvation in the heart of His child, love excels. God's love to us is so precious that we respond to Him in love. This love is the effect of the law written on the tables of our hearts. That law has two parts. It is, first of all, to love God with all our heart, soul, mind, and strength. With God's love in our hearts we worship, honor, and obey Him in love. The law also has a second part, to love our neighbor as ourselves. To fellow believers, this love is demonstrated in the communion of the saints. To neighbors who still are lost in sin, our love to them is expressed in our desire and effort to lead them to salvation.

The effectiveness of the gospel is seen in the life and practice of the members. The marks of the true church become the marks of true Christians as spelled out in the Belgic Confession Article 29. In the earlier part of the article the well-known marks of the true church are mentioned: pure doctrine of the gospel is preached, the sacraments are administered properly, and church discipline is exercised in punishing sin. Then immediately follows the marks of the true Christian.

> With respect to those who are members of the church, they may be known by the marks of Christians, namely, by faith; and when they have received Jesus Christ the only Savior, they avoid sin, follow after righteousness, love the true God and their neighbor, neither turn aside to the right or left, and crucify the flesh with the works thereof.

This is expected of every Christian because God anoints every true believer by His Holy Spirit to serve Him in the church or kingdom of heaven. Every true believer is equipped to be an officebearer in the covenant, a prophet, priest, and king in the service of God.

The Heidelberg Catechism describes this work in Lord's Day 12:

> Why art thou called a Christian? A. Because I am a member of Christ by faith, and thus am partaker of His anointing; that so I may confess His name, and present myself a living sacrifice of thankfulness to Him; and also that with a free and good conscience I may fight against sin and Satan in this life, and afterwards reign with Him eternally over all creatures.

As an anointed prophet, every Christian has the calling and ability to "confess His name." This has many aspects to it. We think of public confession of faith; confessing His name in the instruction of covenant children; and no less importantly, confessing His name to the neighbor, whether Christian or non-Christian. We cannot separate the prophetic office (speech) from the priestly and kingly office (action). Thus the Bible uses the word "conversation," which includes both speech and action. Later the Heidelberg

Catechism, in Lord's Day 32, mentions that by our godly conversation, we may be able "to gain others to Christ."

Witnessing, or the work of evangelism by the members of the church, consists of more than inviting others to come to church. Hearing the preaching of the gospel is the goal of all evangelism. This is necessary because of the key role that Christ has assigned to the preaching of the gospel (Rom. 10:11-15). We may speak of the witnessing of the members as the sharing of the gospel or evangelism because it is in the service of the gospel that they work. Their burden is the salvation of the lost, and this includes bringing them under the preaching of the gospel. To accomplish this, members must realize that for a non-Christian to come under the preaching of the gospel requires our explaining to them what it means to be a Christian, telling them why the gospel is so precious to us, familiarizing them with the Bible, and such things. This is part of our prophetic office, which God may be pleased to use to prepare the heart of one to come under the preaching of the Word.

The benefits of this for the congregation are beyond measure.

True, wrongly motivated and careless methods contribute to the church's fear of such activity. There are many "objections" that have been and are being raised against this activity, which we will address later in this book. But for now we are focusing on the positive, beautiful aspects of witnessing that takes place by individual believers in the church.

Active witnessing on the part of the individual believer contributes in a marvelous way to his own spiritual maturity. Yes, it includes getting sharpened in apologetics, in what to say to those who argue against the gospel and how to give a Christian response to those who deride and mock the gospel. It is much more than that, it relates to the growth of his personal faith. When we witness to others, we have to "walk the talk." Careless living and evangelism are incompatible. We have to know the truth if we are to teach others. We learn quickly that we have to be patient with the spiritual growth of others. We must not be careless in judging and condemning if our goal is to gain others for Christ. In summary, we learn that God saves whom He wills, in the way He wills, and in the time of His own choosing. Nothing quickens the heart more than to be an instrument in the hands of God to lead a lost soul to the Savior. We cannot help but praise God when we see His work of salvation before our very own eyes. At the same time, we learn that we cannot save a soul, it is all of God and all of grace, thus prayer takes on more meaning when we know that the eternal destiny of the souls of those with whom we speak are in God's hands. That is humbling, and that is a good virtue for every Christian.

The church is blessed by such activity. When members of the congregation are involved in personal evangelism, they take an interest in all the mission work of our churches. We appreciate the difficulties involved and are patient and prayerful because we experience it in our own efforts. We want to learn more of what God is doing in the various fields of labor so that we can pray fervently for the Holy Spirit's presence. Even though we live in serious times, the last days, we are not overcome in gloom or defeat by the apostasy within the churches or by the opposition from the world about us. Rather, we remain positive because we are doing the work of our Lord as He has commissioned us to do until He returns. We do not know the day or the hour of His return, so we work fervently and with great hope. His promise is to be with us until the end. The evidence of this is given to us when we recognize His blessings within the congregation and in our evangelistic efforts. This draws us together and makes us joyful and thankful in Him.

# II. Hindrances to This Work

Our emphasis in this book is upon the role of every member of a congregation in the work of evangelism. We made a distinction between the preaching of the gospel in evangelism and the personal witnessing of every believer. These two are clearly taught in the Bible and are important in evangelism. We are now concentrating on the personal witness of every believer and its role in evangelism in the established church. We thereby do not overlook or minimize the importance of the preaching of the gospel; rather, we recognize the supportive role that such witnessing has to the preaching. We emphasized this in the previous section.

As the title of this chapter suggests, we now focus our attention on various issues that arise in connection with personal witnessing. I wondered what to call these "issues." It is possible to view them as obstacles—obstacles that must be overcome if we are actually going to busy ourselves in the important work of personal witnessing. Or, perhaps, we can view them as objections—objections, that is, that are based on biblical principles. The difference between the two is significant. The latter, if indeed they are based on biblical principles, can become more serious. Obstacles, on the other hand, can be overcome, as we allow the Word of God to shed light on the subject at hand. In the end, I opted for a different word. Because I am confident that the positions I take with regard to the issues that arise in connection with personal evangelism are true to the Scriptures, and because I do not imagine them to be so controversial that they will engender "objections," I use the far more optimistic title of hindrances to personal evangelism.

By "hindrances" we mean those issues that can, because of misunderstandings regarding them, get in the way of, or interfere with, our engaging in evangelism as Christ would have us do it. Please note that, in listing them, I am not responding to or reacting against any particular practice or way of thinking in our churches. I present them only as hypothetical problems. In fact, many of them, as I wrote before, have been raised by G. VanDooren, in the book *Get Out*. First, then, we will list the "hindrances," and then provide a response that we believe to be both biblical and in harmony with our confessions.

1. The doctrine of the antithesis forbids us to do personal evangelism with those who differ with us, and even more so with non-Christians. Personal witnessing will involve us in reaching out and befriending our neighbor. If we do this, we will violate the Scripture's teaching of spiritual separation from the world.

2. Our doctrinal beliefs and practices make such attempts at personal evangelism pointless. The doctrine of God's sovereignty and man's depravity are such hindrances that our neighbors are not interested in the Reformed faith. This increases when we add the biblical teaching that rejects labor union membership and divorce and remarriage, to name but two. Paul admitted that the offense of the gospel was great in his day, and we might as well come to terms with this today, since the non-Christian world and the church world have increased in their depravity in these last days of history.

3. We have not emphasized personal evangelism in the past, why do you seem to think it is so important today? Are we not to hold to the "old paths" and warn the people when new ideas are set forth in our churches? Why is this idea of personal witnessing so important all of a sudden?

4. One might say that the critical need we face as churches is to preserve our strength and build one another

18

up spiritually rather than reaching out and trying to bring new converts into the church. Their presence will not make us stronger but weaker. Look at the churches around us that have emphasized evangelism and see how weak they have become. Their evangelism is a contributing factor.

5. I'm not convinced that it is my duty to share the gospel with others. It is the church's duty to preach the gospel, and that is evangelism, period.

6. I lack incentive to speak about my Christian faith to others. If this is true, why should I force myself to do something that isn't there? Are you saying that I lack spirituality and godliness in this regard?

7. Is not our emphasis on the covenant an obstacle to personal evangelism? We emphasize, correctly, the Christian home, the Christian church, and the Christian day school. This makes us introspective and self-focused as people of God. If we do this in obedience to Christ, how are we supposed to reach out to others who do not share this view and who even reject it? Won't we lose our covenantal perspective?

8. Efforts of outreach and evangelism frequently lead to compromise of the gospel and wrong ecumenism. We need but look to other churches for evidence. If we are going to engage in personal witnessing, we are going to be tempted to soften the hard edges of the Reformed faith and make it more attractive so that it will be accepted by more people. This may very well relate to our Reformed distinctives in Christian life as well. Is it not better to be safe than sorry?

9. I don't know what to say or how to evangelize with my neighbors. No one seems interested in teaching me or motivating me, so I just give up. What am I supposed to do?

As you can tell, these are sensitive questions, and questions concerning which there may be differences of opinion. We pose them, not to cause dissension, but to promote understanding, and therefore harmony and unity of purpose in the church of Christ. To that end, I invite response. Responsible exchange of ideas regarding personal evangelism will be helpful, and we can grow together in our understanding of the Word of God and our putting it into practice in evangelism. This can only be helpful and positive in this area of our calling before God. I begin with this confidence and trust in you, the readers.

## First Hindrance

Let's start with the first possible hindrance.

1. The doctrine of the antithesis forbids us to do personal evangelism with those who differ with us, and even more so with non-Christians. Personal witnessing will involve us in reaching out and befriending our neighbor. If we do this, we will violate the Scripture's teaching of spiritual separation from the world.

There are three concepts here that describe our relationship with the non-Christian world around us. We must be careful to understand each one and discern which one correctly describes the biblical teaching of the Christian's place in the world.

The first is "isolation." This view advocates that we must have nothing to do with the world around us. The world is wicked and must be rejected. The Christian must find a retreat and, physically as well as spiritually, put space between himself and the non-Christian. For his own spiritual good, the Christian ought to have no fellowship with the ungodly except what is absolutely necessary for his own survival. This has been the view of those who produced the monasteries and nunneries. This is the world-flight of the Anabaptists, which can be seen in our country in the form of the Amish. The spirit of isolationism encourages Christians to avoid any contact with the world of unbelievers and retreat to covenantal spheres. The battle cry is "in separation there is strength." They mean physical separation, which engenders spiritual separation.

The second view of our relationship with the world is called "synthesis." Supporters of this view suggest that the Christian has to mix in with the ungodly as much as possible in order that his presence may have a spiritual influence upon them for good. The expressed goal is to "Christianize" the world. It is to let one's light shine and thereby improve society by saving souls. There are no real bounds for this activity. In order to lend a godly impact, one can join ungodly organizations, one should send his children to public schools, and Christian teachers ought to penetrate those strongholds of Satan to be like a leaven for moral good. The same applies to our dealings with our non-Christian neighbors. We must get involved with their life and become genuine friends with them, so that the barriers of separation come down and we can influence them with the gospel of truth.

The third view, which I believe is the biblical viewpoint, is called "antithesis." This view rejects both "isolationism" and "synthesis" and advocates a different moral stance toward the world. It is summarized this way: we are in the world but not of the world. There is a distinction made between physical separation and spiritual separation, and it is vitally important, not only to know the difference, but to govern our lives by this difference.

The Bible is clear that we are not to love the world: "Love not the world, neither the things that are in the world. If any man love the world, the love of the Father is not in him" (I

John 2:15). Similarly, "Ye adulterers and adulteresses, know ye not that the friendship of the world is enmity with God? Whosoever therefore will be a friend of the world is the enemy of God" (James 4:4). There are many more passages of the Bible that emphasize such spiritual separation.

When we speak of our sharing the gospel with the non-Christian by befriending him, we have this in mind. We must never deal with our neighbor as if we do not care about our commitment to spiritual separation. All our dealings with personal witnessing must guard against their influencing us with sin. Rather, we seek an opportunity for our influencing them for good.

Let me quote from a few writers who explain this.

> When believers are motivated by a desire for the approval and appreciation of unconverted people and seek to live just as they live, they show they are in love with the world.... The godly man does not turn to the worldly and unconverted for advice, nor does he mix with them in order to identify with them in their behavior, nor yet join in with their bad conversations, Ps. 1:1 Friendship with the world is always on our terms, not theirs (Crossley, *Everyday Evangelism*).

Similarly,

> ...indispensable as penetration is as a prelude to witness, it is no use to have the church identifying with the world if in doing so it ceases to be the church. In a word, identification is not to be identified with assimilation. If salt loses its saltiness, it is useless.... We are to manifest "holy worldliness" because we are called to be "in the world but not of the world" at the same time. We are called to live in natural surroundings a supernatural life to demonstrate in this age of the age to come (John Stott, in his *Our Guilty Silence*).

And one more quote,

> Fundamentally, sanctification is not a matter of geography (where we are) but of the heart (who owns it). A safe distance is maintained as we are constantly transformed by the renewing of our minds, through the truth of God's Word. This requires time alone with Him, when we are actively submitting our minds to the truth. If this practice is not part of our lives, or if it is not effective, we are ill prepared for encounters with non-Christians in the world. In such a case, perhaps isolation would be best after all (Petersen, *Living Proof*).

In review, we are dealing with the first obstacle to effective personal witnessing, which suggests that our befriending non-Christians with a view to influencing them with the gospel is spiritually wrong because we are to be separate from all the wicked and ungodliness. This objection reminds us of the need to be spiritually mature and to guard against such danger, which is that the wicked may have greater influence on us than we may have on them. However, though the danger is real, we may not use that as a reason to have nothing to do with our non-Christian neighbor. Rather, we must examine ourselves and do two things: first, we must recognize that witnessing to him is what God commands us to do, it is God's directive; and second, we must pray that we may be enabled by God's grace to do it properly as unto the Lord, and that the Holy Spirit will bless it unto the heart of the one we seek. Doing this we will be in a spiritual frame of mind and heart to overcome the temptations to stray because of the evil influence of the unsaved neighbor.

It may be helpful if we make a few suggestions on how that may be done. We are not going to develop methodology here. It is our goal to do that in greater detail later on in this book, but here we simply want to illustrate, so that you can better understand what we have in mind, and so that you can rest assured that personal witnessing to non-Christians does not compromise the doctrine of the antithesis.

Foundational to all attempts to witness to the neighbor is our action, how we behave in his presence. This means that we must live holy lives consistently and under all circumstances. It also includes our personal dealings with our neighbor. If we snub him, look the other way, avoid him, refuse to talk to him, we are sending out clear signals that we don't want anything to do with him. If the neighbor picks up on this, he will conclude that we don't care about him at all, about what he does, about what are his values, about what are his struggles in life—nothing. Even if our reason for this attitude is our judgment of him that he is evil and a great sinner before God, such response at this point is wrong because it is premature. We have not attempted to deal with him and his faults in a proper way.

Another action toward the neighbor might be that we jump on him with severe criticism every time we notice that he is doing something we see to be wrong. There is, of course, an important place for correction in the process of evangelism, but we do well to remember that in our initial contacts we ought to hold our mouth until we can build some trust. This is not compromise or unfaithfulness; this is wisdom, as we learn the art of communication and influence.

Rightful action is that we live a holy life as an example of godliness to our neighbor. As we do that, we take a real and sincere interest in his life, his beliefs, his values, his way of living. This means that we develop good communication between ourselves and him. Obviously, this will not be the same with every one of our neighbors; individuals have different personalities and spiritual responses. The point is that if there is a wall of separation between us and our neighbor, it must be because of our neighbor's response to our overtures of the gospel, and not because of the way we treat him. The Bible is full of such caution: "A soft answer turneth away wrath" (Prov. 15:1). "Who is a wise man and endued with knowledge among you? Let him shew out of a good conversation his works with meekness and wisdom" (James 3:13).

This requires of us sincere interest in the person and life of our neighbor. We must build bridges of interest that allow us to demonstrate that we really care about him. These bridges are manifold: simply taking an interest in his life and inquiring of him how things are going, and turning everyday conversations in the direction of spiritual values and Christian response. This can be followed by certain levels of mutual activity. One wonderful way to build bridges is to help him with something that he needs and that we can supply. This demonstrates, both by speech and by action, that we really do care about him and that he can trust us when we talk together of the deeper values of morality and eventually even of faith.

We can be sure that if we do this in the spirit of holiness before God and of love for our neighbor, the right person will be influenced to the glory of God. If the desire of our heart is the conversion of the non-Christian neighbor, if we make that a matter of daily prayer and seek wisdom of God, and if we conduct ourselves with that goal in mind, we can rest assured that his lifestyle and values will not influence us in an evil way. The antithesis will remain in place, and the barrier of spiritual separation will be overcome only when God changes the heart and life of the non-Christian.

## Second Hindrance

Let's now proceed to the second possible obstacle to effective personal witnessing.

25

"2. Our doctrinal beliefs and practices make such attempts at personal evangelism useless. The doctrine of God's sovereignty and man's depravity are such hindrances that our neighbors are not interested in the Reformed faith. This increases when we add the biblical teaching that rejects labor union membership or the forbidding of divorce and remarriage, to name but two. Paul admitted that the offense of the gospel was great in his day, and we might as well come to terms with this today, since the non-Christian world and the church-world have increased in their depravity in these last days of history."

My answer to this proposed obstacle is that it is defeatist and is the devil's delight.

On the surface, and in light of what the Bible says about the increase of sin and apostasy in the church, there seems to be truth to the observation. Hebrews 6 makes a strong statement concerning the inability of an individual to change when that person once knew the truth and experienced personally and close-up the benefits of the gospel, but turned from them. The same applies to churches, as taught in the letters to the seven churches of Asia Minor (Rev. 2 and Rev. 3). The Lord Jesus gives stern warnings that unless they stop their sinful practices and return to Him in obedience, they will perish. America and Europe are full of people who in their generations have had something to do with Christ and His church, but have turned away and now show contempt of their past spiritual training. The explanation for this is not simply human behavior. It is God's judgment upon those who reject Him, even as Jesus instructed His disciples, "And whosoever shall not receive you, nor hear your words, when ye depart out of that house or city, shake off the dust of your feet" (Matt. 10:14). In great measure, this explains why there is precious little fruit upon efforts to convert nominal Christians or those who in their generations knew the way but rejected it.

Even with all this evidence, however, we may never use this knowledge to stop evangelizing as individual Christians or as churches in doing our mission outreach. If we should do that, we step directly into the devil's trap and contradict the direct injunction of our Savior to keep on doing evangelism until He comes again (Matt. 28:18-20). The Word of God does not give us this sober and very realistic assessment of human depravity in order to discourage us from doing Christ's work. Rather He gave that to us so that we would not have an unrealistic goal, which leads to discouragement and defeat. All outreach, evangelism, and mission work is hard work and, humanly speaking, impossible. The more we realize this, the more we approach it in a proper spiritual way and get on our knees to seek divine help, for without it all our labors are in vain. The salvation of a soul, the gathering of the church, is God's work through Jesus Christ alone.

There is also, in this proposed obstacle, an inherent fallacy, that a duty assigned can be terminated by negative results. One of the great evils in the church today is that methodology in the work of the church is determined by results. If it works, it must be good; if it doesn't work, we need to change it. See the sad results of this kind of reasoning as it is applied to the worship service. Everything, from the informal dress, to the singing, to the casual environment, to the entertainment that replaces preaching, is justified because this is what people want. We must not be drawn into the temptation to abandon the work of the gospel because no one seems interested or because very few respond. Nor must we be tempted to change the contents of the gospel in order to make it more appealing to the general public. These evil responses may result if we suggest in any way that it is useless to spread the gospel because hardly anyone cares anymore to listen.

Rather, we do well to take a serious look at the gospel that constitutes the good news that we bear in our personal witnessing and our preaching. The Bible is the revelation of God, and whatever God says in His Word is the message that we bring to others. The great theme of the Bible is the majesty, sovereignty, and glory of God. In no other book, and from no other source, is there such knowledge of the one true and only living God. Yes, His handiwork, creation, testifies of His excellent glory and power to such a degree that if that is all any man receives from Him, it is sufficient for God to judge him and hold him accountable for all his sinful actions (Rom. 1:18-21). As beautiful and powerful as the testimony of creation is concerning God, however, its message cannot and does not save the sinner. In the immediately preceding verses (Rom. 1:1-17), Paul expresses this. The power of God unto salvation is in the gospel that he preached. In the gospel the righteousness of God is revealed, and in such a way that righteousness is necessary for salvation, for it replaces the unrighteousness of man. That ability to be right with God is merited by Jesus Christ through His death and resurrection, and is appropriated by faith alone. The only escape from the wrath of God is in Jesus Christ. Reconciliation with God and the peace that follows is the good news of the gospel.

I urge you, dear reader, not to discredit the good news of the gospel because it lacks public support or popular appeal. If God has saved you, you will recognize with grateful heart that your salvation is the most wonderful act of God's mercy to you, an undeserving sinner. Eternal predestination is the sweet fountain of God's love, from which flows every blessing of salvation. Christ's death on the cross is not a divine atrocity; rather, it is the supreme expression of love and reconciliation to all who believe. You will also come to realize that holy living is not an oppressive burden to be borne under a severe Master. No, it is as Jesus said, "My yoke is easy and my burden is light" (Matt. 11:28-30). When divine grace flows from a sanctified heart and affects the very being of a converted sinner, it is supreme delight to be spared sin and its consequences and to be brought into a liberty and freedom within the boundaries of God's law and Scripture. Just because many around you do not care about the gospel or express offense in its message does not take away from the fact that you know the beauty of its truth and enjoy the power of its deliverance. God expects you to understand this, and, out of an obedient heart and with the motive of love and joy to Him, to take up your calling to evangelize with thanksgiving.

There is a conclusion that we can draw from all of this. God is able to change hearts and save souls. He never promises to save the masses. His promise is that, "as many as were ordained to eternal life believed" (Acts 13:48). "The Lord added to the church daily such as should be saved" (Acts 2:47). We must not decide whether we will evangelize our non-Christian neighbor on the basis of whether we think he is savable or whether we think that there might be some hope of changing him. If we do this, we are doomed before we start. The question is not whether we think it can be done, but it is whether God is pleased to accomplish it. With this approach we never pre-judge anyone as to the possible outcome. We simply speak of the wonderful works of God, and in humility and in prayer seek God's blessing to work in such a heart if it pleases Him.

This will keep us both optimistic and humbly dependent on Him. We may even learn that the one we thought least likely is just the one God is pleased to save. He does this so that all the glory of such salvation is His alone and not ours. Paul concludes his teaching of this great truth in Romans 11:36: "For of him, and through him, and to him, are all things: to whom be glory for ever. Amen."

## Third Hindrance

We now focus our attention on the third proposed hindrance to personal evangelism.

3. We have not emphasized personal evangelism in the past. Why do we seem to think it is so important today? Are we not to hold to the "old paths" and warn the people when new ideas are set forth in our churches? Why is this idea of personal witnessing so important all of a sudden?

The place to begin addressing this concern is the question whether personal evangelism is in fact something new. Is personal witnessing by the believer a new practice, and, if so, to whom is it new?

If we survey briefly the history of the Christian church, we would have to conclude that personal witnessing has always been part of the life of the membership. As we noted before, it is set forth in the New Testament as the normal behavior of all new converts who have been brought to true faith. This relates to the shepherds who worshiped the newborn King (Luke 2:17, 18); the Samaritan woman (John 4:28ff.); the persecuted saints of the early Christian church (Acts 8:4); and the Christians who were scattered abroad and needed to be reminded that by holy living they had the privilege of evangelizing personally (I Pet. 3:15, 16).

The church took seriously the need to instruct her members to live a godly life and to evangelize others, as is evident in the church of Philadelphia. Christ said to her, in the letter addressed to her in Revelation 3:7-14, that she had "kept my word and hast not denied my name," and "thou has kept the word of my patience." How did she do this? The angel of this church certainly set forth the word of truth and taught it to the congregation by the preaching of the gospel. The people in turn received it and broadcasted it. This is why Christ said she had an "open door." The promise that Christ gave to her is that her enemies would "come and worship before thy feet." Christ would give them amazing success in their outreach ministry. Such activity would not weaken the church. It will have the opposite effect: "Him that overcometh will I make a pillar in the temple of my God."

The history of the Reformation demonstrates as well that the ordinary members of the church received the grace of God to confess shamelessly and openly the truth of the gospel as it was delivered unto them through the Reformation. This activity played a key role in the amazing speed with which the truth spread throughout all the countries of Europe. This was true even in the face of the cruelest opposition. They were eager to speak to others of the gospel of salvation by grace through faith. Personal evangelism was used by God at great expense to the faithful—and with mighty success.

The history of mission work by the church illustrates this fact over and over. God raised up fearless preachers to travel throughout the world to preach the great gospel of justification by faith alone. Missionaries brought the same message with the same courage. They did this at the time of the Reformation already and carried on the work all through the church's history. Also in missions, the new believers responded to the Word preached and spoke to others of their newfound joy. This contributed to the formation of the church everywhere. Story after story can be told of the lone missionary who worked diligently for years until the Lord gave him his first convert. Then things would change. God by the Holy Spirit raised up a new convert, a local person, who was changed from heathendom to the Christian faith. Usually, this person formed the necessary bridge to reach out to the community so that others eventually joined with them in worship and the formation of a church.

The establishing of a church does not mean that this outreach of personal evangelism may then stop. God's instruction is clear: it must continue. In the way of such activity the Lord adds new members through the wonder of conversion. These new converts are encouraged by the godly example of mature Christians who had the benefit of covenant instruction all their lives. Baptism of adults blends beautifully with the baptism of infants as God gathers His church in the local congregation.

These are the "old paths" that we must acknowledge as right for the church and ought to be part of the life of everyone in our congregations. I am so convinced of this, that if you ask me what one thing is necessary if our churches will be truly mission-minded churches, I would answer that it is the personal evangelism by every member. If we do this in obedience to the instruction of the Word of God, every member will be mission-minded, and outreach, love, and care for others will be the experience of all of us. This will engender in us a true love for the lost souls that God may be pleased to save through us. And out of this personal involvement will also come a desire to do this "with the churches in common" in areas far removed and in foreign settings that require mutual cooperation. Each one of us will appreciate the difficulties connected with mission work from our own experience. It will drive us to our knees to seek God's blessing of courage and strength. All our members need a "heart for missions," which can come only when we are personally obedient to Christ in doing evangelism where He has placed us.

From some points of view this is new for us, and it is probably for that reason that it becomes a hindrance to personal witnessing. It is not true that personal witnessing on the part of our membership was completely lacking in the past or that it was forbidden. It is more correct to say that it was not given its proper emphasis. There are many reasons for this. Some of these reasons I have mentioned before and need not repeat. Most of them pertain to our history and the priority given to combating error, advancing covenant instruction, dealing with the practical applications of covenant truth, and such like. In the midst of this we did put forth efforts for mission work and God blessed these as well. The emphasis correctly was placed upon the preaching of the gospel as God's way to gather the church. Also this was done to combat the errors prevalent in the evangelical church world that contented itself with self-made missionaries. It is time now to emphasize the equally biblical truth that every believer has the gifts and calling to evangelize through personal witnessing. A good and healthy emphasis on personal evangelism within the established church will help us to reach outside of the comforts of our covenant sphere and let our light shine in the world beyond, as Christ has instructed us to do.

## Fourth Hindrance

4. One might say that the critical need we face as churches is to preserve our strength and build one another up spiritually rather than reaching out and trying to bring new converts into the church. Their presence will not make us stronger but weaker. Look at the churches around us that have emphasized evangelism. See how weak they have become. Their evangelism is a contributing factor.

We have to address two aspects of this question: First, if a member of the church practices personal evangelism, this activity will not weaken his spiritual life but strengthen it; and second, if our churches handle properly the increase of membership that results from conversion, it will not weaken our congregations but strengthen them. Let's see how this is true.

We face real spiritual dangers if we maintain a life of isolation, that is, if we literally separate ourselves from the world around us and have little or nothing to do with our neighbors. These dangers are threefold: first, the danger of self-righteousness. This evil is always associated with self-centeredness. I will then look at myself as the standard of all good, both as pertains to faith and life. Everyone who does not measure up to me must be rejected, and everyone who agrees with me is my friend. Second, isolation produces ignorance of the real world around us and allows us to function in a make-believe world. Our effectiveness as

Christians in dealing with our neighbors, so that we can let our light shine to them, is dependent on whether or not we understand their world. The spirit of isolation prevents us from doing this. Finally, isolation produces a spirit of combativeness in us that hinders rather than helps us in our calling to witness to the non-Christian neighbor. Our view of spiritual warfare becomes a barrage of name-calling and judgmental verdicts, which erect barriers impossible to overcome. We hardly ever ask ourselves if our conduct hinders our opportunity to interact with the neighbor and, if God be willing, to lead him to Christ.

If we engage in personal evangelism, we will develop spiritual strengths that overcome these weaknesses. We can list four of them. First, we will develop our ability really to love our neighbor as God commands us to do. In love we will actually look upon a non-Christian neighbor with sadness of heart. We will feel a burden for the children that are raised in that non-Christian home. It is good for us to sit down and ask ourselves, as a family, how we can reach out to them. Yes, we can easily judge them, for they have all sorts of wrongs in their life. Rather, we will set that aside for the time being in order that we may introduce them to something far better. Most of the members of the congregation already have this love for other members. They must learn to show love also to those outside the church. Second, we rejoice in God's sovereignty over all of life, including salvation. Personal evangelism gives us the opportunity to experience God's sovereignty as He works through us in a non-Christian. We learn to focus on the most important message, repentance of sin and faith in Jesus Christ as the way to the Father. No one can keep the law unless he or she comes to know the Lawgiver. God alone is able to bring about that change. When you do personal evangelism, you see little glimmers of that divine work, and your appreciation for and dependency on God skyrockets. Third, your personal faith will grow as you share the gospel with someone who knows not God. This applies to all aspects of truth, both doctrinal and practical. Does personal evangelism weaken the membership? That charge can only be raised out of ignorance. Finally, our devotional life will come alive because our personal and family prayer life will also focus on the spiritual progress of a neighbor or relative who is important to us and we desire his salvation. Only God can do that, and we learn to wait upon Him. That is wonderful spiritual maturity.

The second aspect of this hindrance is the fear that if God blesses the efforts of personal evangelism, it will weaken our churches because these people will not be really Protestant Reformed and they will bring into our midst all sorts of issues of doctrines and lifestyles, and that will not be good.

This is a legitimate concern, because, as the proposed hindrance states, many churches have been weakened, and apostasy prevails, because of such evangelism. You must realize, however, that wrongful dealing with converts must not deter us from doing it properly, and we must not use improper evangelism by others as a scare-tactic to prevent our members from doing what God commands us to do. Humanly speaking, there is always a measure of "risk" in evangelism because we can never be sure what God is going to do in the life of non-Christians or what impact their presence might have upon us or the membership. But fear of wrongful influence from their presence must not deter us from doing the work God commands us to do. Rather we must take an honest look at ourselves if we are afraid of such influence. Are we so weak or so vulnerable to wrongful influence that we conclude that we will succumb to tempta-tion because God places immature or inquiring sinners in our midst? Perhaps we should look at it from a different point of view and ask ourselves, could some of our members be an offense to them, because what we teach newcomers is not always what our members practice. You see, wrongful influence goes both ways. That would be sad indeed if our spirituality has come to such a low.

We must ask the question, is the congregation weakened by the presence of a person or family who is showing interest in the gospel and seeks to worship God and fellowship with His people? Obviously, our answer will be determined by our judgment of these people. If we are so naïve spiritually that we will not tolerate in our midst anyone who is not Protestant Reformed in confession and life (on the level of our own spiritual maturity), then of course their mere presence is threatening and we would judge that our congregation is at risk just because they are there. If we have developed a proper tolerance for people who are inquiring and seeking after God, but have not yet attained and are willing to learn about the Christian faith and life, our perspective is not that of weakness due to their presence but opportunity to serve and glorify God through them.

A number of things must be said to safeguard faithfulness to God in the process of evangelism.

We must encourage one another that befriending non-Christians does not mean that we allow them to influence us in a sinful way. If we do this, then the devil has the last laugh after all. Spiritual separation means that we develop a careful balance between befriending them as a way to share the gospel with them and being careful not to compromise our own faith. The individual members of the congregation must be challenged to evangelize, that is, to bring these strangers and foreigners into the household of faith so they believe and live as we do. The task of members does not end when one member brings an inquirer into the fellowship of the church. No, it is then that the entire congregation has to reach out to such a one. Each member now has the opportunity to use his own gifts to make this person or family feel at home, to enjoy contact with covenant homes and schools, and to see Christian life from the inside. I do not say that everyone must rush out to do this all at once, for then the inquirer may very well be scared off. Rather this is a process of time, and every member must know it his duty eventually to be involved in this activity.

We must also put in place a method of instruction, so that such inquirers can be thoroughly trained in the truth of the Reformed faith and holy living. Such careful instruction takes time and effort and must not be neglected, for therein lies the answer to the threat of the weakening of the church. We have a thorough program of instruction for covenant children, for young adults and families. It may be that new converts do not fit into this structure at all and that it is time we set in place individual classes for such people. This is less intimidating, more personal, and can be better adapted to their needs.

Personal evangelism is our calling, and we must prayerfully seek not only to do it, but also to put into place the follow-up that is necessary for a strong church.

## Fifth Hindrance

We direct our attention now to the fifth proposed hindrance to personal evangelism.

> 5. I'm not convinced that it is my duty to share the gospel with others. It is the church's duty to preach the gospel and this is evangelism, period.

We have already addressed different aspects of this hindrance in this book and do not need to repeat them here. We wrote an entire section on "The Role of Every Believer in Evangelism." We also expanded on this in our answer to the third hindrance, which concerned the present-day emphasis upon personal evangelism when it seemed dormant in the past.

It might be helpful, however, if we add a few more passages from the Bible that focus upon the duty of every Christian to share the gospel with others. These we glean from the book of G. VanDooren *Get Out*, chapter 5. He makes the pertinent observation that our duty as individual Christians stands at the bottom of a list that astounds us. God Himself proclaimed the gospel in paradise. Then He sent angels and prophets. In the fullness of time He sent His own Son to make the Father known. After Him the Holy Spirit came to convince the world of sin and salvation. The apostles became His instruments and established churches; they were the gift of Christ to the saints (Eph. 4). And finally, we appear on the scene as the royal priesthood of God to proclaim His praises.

We are at the bottom. But let's not minimize our calling. God could have easily done without us. But He did not and He does not. VanDooren then borrows from John Stott's booklet, *Our Guilty Silence*, these references. I Peter 2:5, 9 is a reference to God's people as a holy priesthood. In verse 5, Peter calls us "to offer up spiritual sacrifices acceptable to God by Christ Jesus." This is our worship. In verse 9 he adds, "that ye should shew forth the praises of him who hath called you out of darkness into his marvelous light." This "shew forth" is not limited to our worship. It is the word for evangelism. It is "to tell forth or to show forth." Worship and witness go together. There are places in the New Testament where believers are called "witnesses" or "fountains of living waters" (Acts 1:8; John 4:14; John 7:37-39). Philippians 2:15, 16 is special. Paul reminds us of our calling to live antithetically, "be blameless ... in the midst of a crooked and perverse nation," but he also adds, "among whom ye shine as lights in the world." We do this by "holding forth the Word of life." We ought to note that the word is not "holding fast" but "holding forth," the difference being obvious. The purpose is to be a godly witness to those who are without the congregation.

38

Jesus said concerning His disciples, "As thou hast sent me into the world, even so have I also sent them into the world" (John 17:18; John 20:21). This is an injunction to the disciples as they represented the church. In them the entire church is comprehended, so we may conclude that Christ Jesus sends office bearers to preach the gospel in their capacity and office, but through them He sends the entire church to witness concerning the same gospel. A good example of this is given in John 13:34, 35: "A new commandment I give unto you that ye love one another; as I have loved you, that ye also love one another. By this shall all men know that ye are my disciples, if ye have love one to another." Our witness as members of the congregation is directed to the whole world, and it is so important that it confirms the gospel of love that is preached in the local church.

Along this same line, if we compare John 1:18 with I John 4:12 we get the same idea. "No man hath seen God at any time; the only begotten Son, which is in the bosom of the Father, he hath declared him" (John 1:18). I John 4:12 adds, "No man hath seen God at any time. If we love one another, God dwelleth in us, and his love is perfected in us." Now the Father can be seen by others through us by our words of witness: "we have seen and do testify that the Father sent the Son to be the Savior of the world" (I John 4:14), and by our action, "Herein is our love made perfect, that we may have boldness in the day of judgment: because as he is, so are we in this world" (I John 4:17). This witness of love encompasses our speech, which is confirmed by our actions.

## Sixth Hindrance

6. I lack incentive to speak about my Christian faith to others. If this is true, why should I force myself to do something that isn't there? Are you saying that I lack spirituality and godliness in this regard?

The lack of desire to witness concerning our great God and His Son Jesus Christ is rooted in our own spiritual apathy. The Old Testament word for prophet is to boil over. The idea is that the spiritual life of God, worked in us, is like an artesian well that has natural force from within to spew water out of the ground. Our God is wonderful. He is the only God. And to live apart from Him is *death*. Our only comfort in life and death is to shout, I am not my own, but I belong to my faithful Savior Jesus Christ. He alone satisfied for all my sins, and He is the One who conquered the devil and all his hosts so that I am safe from all his wiles. Not a hair can fall from my head without Father's will because of Jesus. Our Belgic Confession develops this faith in such a way that God triune is acknowledged as God, and His work of creation and recreation is in Jesus Christ His Son and applied by the Holy Spirit. Our Canons of Dordt extol God's sovereignty in salvation, which is from eternity to eternity. Every teaching of these confessions is derived from the Holy Scriptures and has stood the test of history. This is truth, God's truth, the truth whereby man may be saved. Precious few people or churches hold to them anymore today. These confessions express the complete doctrine of salvation. Witnessing to non-Christians is the blessed activity of a living Christian whose faith is real and dynamic and who earnestly desires to share it with others.

If anyone lacks zeal for this great work, that person is like a mother who says to her children, "I don't feel like rearing you in the fear of God anymore, I don't have the incentive." If you ask me whether this is due to her lack of spirituality and godliness, my answer would be, "Yes, I am sorry for her, her great privilege to be a godly mother is ruined by her spiritual indifference, which contributes to her lack of zeal and joy to do this work." The same is true for any Christian who complains of lack of zeal to witness to others. The reason has to be sought from within: Why does not the fountain of living water produce a well, springing up unto everlasting life (John 4:14)? There may be many contributing factors, far too many to deal with here in this brief answer. You must be clear that indifference towards witnessing for the gospel is a spiritual malady that must be addressed with the earnestness of prayer and the Word of God.

## Seventh Hindrance

> 7. Is not our emphasis on the covenant an obstacle to personal evangelism? We emphasize correctly the impor-tance of the Christian home, the Christian church, and the Christian day school. This makes us introspective and self-focused as people of God. If we do this in obedience to Christ, how are we supposed to reach out to others who do not share this view and who even reject it? Won't we lose our covenant perspective?

Rather than viewing our use of separate institutions (especially Christian schools) as a hindrance, we ought to view it as an advantage. Yes, obviously every neighbor is not going to appreciate this separateness, especially when you tell them how much it costs. As Reformed believers we are not recluses, nor are our churches, homes, and schools perpetuating a notion of "other worldliness" that makes our next generation ineffective in their place in the world. We could do this if we emphasize isolation rather than antith-esis. But we thank God that this is not the case. We and our children live in this world and have a calling to interact with this world, but not to partake of their worldly behavior or character. The covenant emphasis that we enjoy, on the basis of the Bible, is that we walk with our God in every activity. This marks us as Christian, and we will not com-promise our convictions of faith and practice.

Such Christians are not a detriment to society; they make the best citizens in every aspect. We are honest workers, trustworthy in business, we are not so driven by free enterprise that we undercut all competition and have as our goal to become millionaires. Rather we are good stewards of everything God has entrusted to us and know that the profit of our labor is for the benefit of others as well as ourselves. Every profession is a calling to serve God in the midst of society. We do this by loving God and our neighbor. This is a high calling and we honor God this way. Our witness by our daily Christian activity does not come about because we are better than others in ourselves. It is the product of God's sovereign grace and mercy given to us and strengthened through the blessings of the covenant church, home, and school. When we live like a Christian in every profession to which God calls us, we are ready to confirm that walk of faith with our godly testimony and witness. The reason for our joyful walk of faith in every circumstance, in prosperity and adversity, is our God and His love for us.

If we take this approach, our covenantal blessings will not deter us from reaching out or tempt us to abandon them, but rather encourage us to appreciate these blessings and be ready to share them with others. Again, we cannot prejudge whether others will care about it, respond appreciatively, or mock us. This is in God's hands. One thing is for sure, we don't have to hold back because of our faith and understanding of God's covenant. As Reformed believers, our goal is not simply to "save souls" but to bring souls into God's covenant, including the church, home, and school. We can hold our heads high in thanksgiving to God for giving us such spiritual blessings. What a thrill it is when others receive eyes to see and hearts to believe such a wonderful truth. The evidence of grace is that they quickly learn to appreciate this covenant life.

## Eighth Hindrance

8. Efforts of outreach and evangelism frequently lead to compromise of the gospel and wrongful ecumenism. We

need but look to other churches for evidence. If we are going to engage in personal witnessing, we are going to be tempted to soften the hard edges of the Reformed faith and make it more attractive so that it will be accepted by more people. This may very well relate to our Reformed distinctives in Christian life as well. Is it not better to be safe than sorry?

This question is similar to one we answered before, so we can be brief. If safety means that we neglect our calling to do what God has commanded us to do, we are pretending to be wiser than God. Our supposed safety is wrongfully conceived. Here too the danger of isolation lurks in the background. Such isolation boasts, "in separation is our strength," and when this is perceived to be physical separation and non-engagement with the world around us, we fail to let our light shine.

We do well to recognize that there are dangers in heeding the biblical injunction to do personal evangelism and witnessing. Engagement with non-Christians carries with it dangers and temptations. The Word of God makes clear that just because a divine calling carries with it dangers due to engagement (notably our calling to do spiritual warfare with the devil and his hosts, Ephesians 6), we are not instructed to disengage but to engage in battle properly, by wearing God's armor and earnest prayer. Any interaction with non-Christians occasions temptations that we either go softly to the point of compromise or go so far as to please others so that we yield to their ways. This is not cause to cease from such important work, rather it is a clear warning that we take up this task with much prayer and study of God's Word, imploring the Holy Spirit to accompany our every effort.

As noted above, if we truly love God's Word and its precious teaching of truth and practice, we will not give this up under any circumstance. History shows that when persecution became the worst, faith manifested itself the strongest. This was true, even unto death. This didn't just happen, this was God's way of taking care of His people who preached and witnessed to a cruel world that did not want their testimony. God's gift of faith to them was so great that they were able to endure or overcome anything that man gave them (Heb. 11). Unfaithful men and women were always present in the church, but they received their reward from a just God. Their compromise never prevented the faithful from serving their God with thanksgiving. It must not do this in our day either.

## Ninth Hindrance

9. I don't know what to say or how to evangelize with my neighbors. No one seems interested in teaching me or motivating me so I just give up. What am I supposed to do?

This is an excellent example of "blame shifting." It is wonderful if you have parents who will help you, if you have a church that pays attention to this need, or if you can reach out to those around you and get help and encouragement. Fact is that if God by His Holy Spirit impresses on you the duty and privilege to engage in personal witnessing to those around you, you can do something about it right now.

First, examine your motive why you have this desire. Is it from a heart that truly loves God and your neighbor and not because you are out to prove yourself as a Christian. Do you really desire the salvation of your neighbor or are you out to win an argument. There is a big difference—one is carnal the other is spiritual.

Second, begin by engaging in talk with those neighbors with whom you come into contact. Begin by neighborly talk and put forth effort to turn this conversation into a spiritual direction. Just try it and become familiar with this experience. This will help you to be motivated to pursue your desire so that you will not be easily discouraged and quit.

Third, get some good reading material on this subject. I mentioned some books earlier. If you cannot form judgment on whether a certain book is reliable material or not, ask your pastor or elder to help you.

Fourth, find likeminded Christians and join together for study, encouragement, mutual activity, and prayer in order to help each other in this important effort. Call it a small support group, whatever, this can be decisive for you, because it may be very discouraging to do it all alone. Best of all, one or two fellow members of your congregation who share this desire can do it together. You will find it exciting to grow in your faith and practice in witnessing for the gospel.

May God use this chapter to motivate and enable us to overcome any hindrance so that we can engage in personal evangelism as we witness concerning our God and His Son, our Savior, Jesus Christ. May your efforts be blessed by Him.

# III. Sharing the Good News

We ought to pause a moment to get our bearing as to where we are going in this book. The general theme is "Personal Evangelism." We are considering this subject in connection with the efforts of each local church to do outreach ministry. Our contention is that any such effort must include and emphasize the importance of personal evangelism by the members of the congregation. In the first chapter we set forth the legitimacy of the activity within the office of believer: Every member of the church has the calling and qualification to share his faith with others. Then we spent a lengthy chapter addressing a series of nine hindrances or obstacles that have to be overcome if we are going to practice this calling among us. We now want to direct our attention to the positive side—that is, how we can go about doing this work and what we must keep in mind in actually engaging in personal evangelism. We begin this by considering what it is that we share when we personally evangelize. The answer is simply, we share the good news of the gospel.

Two things have to be said at this point.

First, please remember that by expressing it this way we do not in any way minimize the importance of the preaching of the gospel. This seems to be the biggest difficulty we face in giving a proper place to personal evangelism. I would think that in light of what we have written in the past, this ought to be acceptable to our readers. The preaching of the gospel is God's way of declaring the good news of salvation to everyone, whether in the local church or on the mission field. It is because of the wonderful work of the Holy Spirit through the preached word that the believers who embrace this word are equipped to take the word preached and function in their office of believer and practice personal evangelism. Also, the great goal of personal evangelism is to excite others to come and hear the preaching of the Word in the established church. Personal evangelism is no threat to the preaching of the gospel. It depends upon it and expands its usefulness outside the walls of the congregation. We have cited enough passages from the Bible in our past writings so that we can now move on.

Secondly, as we say something about the content of the gospel, the good news that is shared with others by our personal evangelism, we must of necessity be brief. We speak of everything we learn from our pastors as they preach to us every Lord's Day. We grow through our own reading of the Bible and personal study. We talk about our faith with fellow Christians and members of the congregation and learn from their experiences how the Bible speaks to them and how they apply it to their own lives as children of God. We ask, what do we say to non-Christians, nominal Christians, or even weak and seeking Christians, when we share with them the gospel? The broad answer is: everything that God gives to us in the Bible and that forms for us the basis of the good news that means so much to us personally. We want, now, to condense and simplify this knowledge so that we can better witness personally to others.

For our encouragement, we are among the most equipped and blessed people on the face of the earth to know what to say. There are precious few churches that have such a solid catechism program, Bible Study meetings for every age, and good preaching on the Lord's Day as we have as churches. Our members, including our youth, have every advantage to know and appreciate the gospel. Even controversy has sharpened our knowledge in areas of doctrine and life. What a difference there is between us and new converts who have opportunity personally to evangelize and do their best with their limited knowledge and experience. We do not say that they are not qualified to do this, because then we deny God's work in them, and experience testifies the opposite. In their "first love", God enables them to reach out to others and be a blessing to bring into the church many other non-Christians. From the point of view of ability to know what to say and how to express it, we have some advantage over them. This ought to encourage us to press on with the task. They have the advantage of "first love" motivation, which most of us lack. Our difficulty and lack is the motivation to go out and do it. This is why new converts in the midst of the congregation are such a blessing and motivation for us all.

Where do we start when we have the opportunity to share the good news of the gospel with someone who is not a Christian? Let's just give a few highlights.

First, we must begin with God!

The Bible does this: "In the beginning *God*...." The good news of the gospel is all about our God. The world is full of false gods. As we do personal evangelism, we do not have to take up controversy with those around us first thing. If we are truly converted to God, we have in our hearts an excitement of who our God is. We cannot help but speak to others about all His wonderful works. "Many, O Lord my God, are thy wonderful works ... if I would declare and speak of them, they are more than can be numbered" (Ps. 40:5). I recall during a visit to India that we had opportunity on a Sunday morning to speak about our God as a Friend (something quite foreign to any other god). The occasion was our praying together in a local coffee shop during breakfast and a local Muslim came up and asked if we were Christians. He wanted to speak with us. We talked for over an hour with him about who our God really is. That is where the gospel begins.

You may ask, should we not begin by pointing out that a non-Christian is a sinner in need of Jesus? The answer is that such a person will never know his sins, unless he stands before the God of the Bible. People have so many ideas about sin; even heathen people do, and they quite often speak about hell for sinners. When we share the gospel with non-Christians (and even other Christians who are not Reformed) the issue is always, who is God. When we speak about the holiness and justice of God as set forth in the Bible, such a person begins to realize that the one true God is pure and cannot tolerate any sin. God defines what sin is, and we stand before Him as if we are in His courtroom and He is the judge who makes such determination.

This is done so effectively in Romans. After the greeting, Paul expresses to the Roman Christians his desire to bring the gospel to them, and he details that gospel in terms of the "righteousness of God" (Romans 1:17). Furthermore, he defines the heart of the gospel in terms of justification by faith (Romans 1:17). He does not hesitate, then, to speak of the wrath of God upon the wicked, pointing out that idolatry is not ignorance but conscious rejection of the God revealed in creation, and therefore they are accountable to Him even though they wallow in their immorality, including homosexuality (Romans 1:20-32).

This is also done in our Heidelberg Catechism. I have already used Romans as the biblical basis for "proofing" the Catechism, because it follows the same pattern as the Catechism. I know my comfort, so as to live and die happily, in the threefold knowledge of how great my sins and miseries are, how I am delivered from my sins in Christ, and how I shall express my gratitude towards God for that deliverance. If you examine the Catechism in the first part, man's sinfulness is determined by God Himself. God is the One who defines sin, and not just as a few wrongful deeds, but as sinfulness rooted in our fallen human nature.

Second, the important link between sharing the virtues and praises of God and confronting the sinner with his guilt before God is the sovereignty of God. The Reformed faith is so helpful in this regard. You need but speak a few moments with a non-Christian about God and sin and he will

50

soon make this point: "Why should I accept your God as telling me what to do? I have my own religion; you have yours. Nice to meet you!" The answer to that is God's sovereignty, though we might not want to use that word, because the non-Christian would not understand it. We have to press on with this observation, that God has the right to expect every human being to behave himself on His terms and to define sin according to His standard, because He has created the universe and preserves every human being. We must point out that we are talking to each other this very moment because of God's care.

Now is the time to focus on the origin of man and how God created him. This God is so great that He not only made the first man and woman, but continues providentially to keep the universe in place. God made the first couple perfect and without sin. Man voluntarily disobeyed God, even after God had warned him, "the day that thou eatest thereof, thou shalt surely die." Adam represented every human being, hence God's punishment justly falls on everyone of us. Romans 5:12, "Wherefore, as by one man sin entered into the world, and death by sin; and so death passed upon all men, for that all have sinned." From that moment on, the human race became spiritual enemies of God, lovers of pleasure, as described in Romans 1:20-32. Their very nature became, as the Catechism says, "incapable of doing any good and inclined to all evil." God had every right to punish the entire human race with physical death at that moment, "for all have sinned and come short of the glory of God" (Rom. 3:23). He could have destroyed the heaven and earth right then and there. But He did not. Why not? The answer is that He willed to save a people whom He had chosen in Jesus Christ His Son. He had planned, even before He had created man, that man would fall into sin; but, more than that, He also planned a way of salvation. With His eye upon saving His people, God preserves the universe and keeps every natural law in place. We owe our existence to Him who is the Lord of the universe.

51

He has the right to tell us how to live and to call us to account.

Third, Jesus is God's Son, whom He gave to die on the cross to satisfy His own justice and merit forgiveness. Romans 6:23: "For the wages of sin is death; but the gift of God is eternal life through Jesus Christ our Lord." Also, "But God commendeth his love toward us, in that, while we were yet sinners, Christ died for us" (Rom. 5:8). This is the heart of the good news of the gospel. Because there is among many heathen religions mention of gods having a family and sending family members to earth to do all sorts of things with mankind, this can easily be confused as just another such narrative. The emphasis here must be on the unique way in which God sent His Son. He Fathered Him by means of a virgin, so that His Son was both God and man. This was necessary, as His work on earth was to make payment for man's sins, and the debt of sin was everlasting punishment in hellfire. The cross has a wonder about it in that it is not just a story of a good man who was made the victim by evil men, but it is God's cross. He willed that His Son be on that cross as the only way in which He could put on His Son His just wrath for the sins of His people. God gave His own Son as the substitute in place of man, who could never bear it. This sets forth the amazing depth of God's love for His children; He punished His Son in order to spare us. The resurrection becomes, then, the confirmation on God's part that His Son bore this punishment and God was satisfied. The cross reveals both justice and mercy or love in amazing harmony.

Fourth, our proper response to this wonderful work of God in giving us His Son is to acknowledge our sins by repentance (heartfelt sorrow and desire to forsake them) and to embrace Jesus Christ as our Savior and Lord. Romans 4:25; Romans 5:1: "Who was delivered for our offenses, and was raised again for our justification. Therefore being justified by faith, we have peace with God through our Lord Jesus Christ." At this point, the great truth of our justification by God through faith must be set forth. Justification is of great value because it establishes the legal basis for our being adopted as God's children and enjoying the benefits of forgiveness of sin and everlasting inheritance. The condemned sinner must hear from God the Judge that he is righteous by means of his faith in Jesus. He is not righteous on the basis of his faith, because faith is God's wonderful gift to us by grace (Eph. 2:8-10). Faith is the means or the tool that God uses to join us to His Son Jesus Christ, and through that union imparts to us the benefits of His suffering and death.

That faith includes our active response to the call of the gospel. Romans 10:9, 10: "That if thou shalt confess with thy mouth the Lord Jesus, and shalt believe in thine heart that God hath raised him from the dead, thou shalt be saved. For with the heart man believeth unto righteousness; and with the mouth confession is made unto salvation." For this reason, in our presentation of the gospel, the matter of confession of the Lord Jesus must not be simply stated as a fact (abstractly as a biblical teaching), but must be set forth as an urgent and necessary response. To our listener, our personal witnessing does not differ one bit from the call of the gospel set forth in the preaching of the gospel as far as the message is concerned. The difference is that in the preaching Christ Himself addresses the sinner; in our personal evangelism we share the message as we talk about God and His Son, Jesus. This is why we want to lead a seeking soul to the feet of Jesus, who speaks in the midst of His church by the word preached.

Finally, what is a proper response to God for this salvation? It is a thankful and obedient life. Romans 13:8-10: "Owe no man anything, but to love one another; for he that loveth another hath fulfilled the law. For this, Thou shalt not commit adultery, thou shalt not kill, thou shalt not steal, thou shalt not bear false witness, thou shalt not covet, and if there be any other commandment, it is briefly comprehended in this saying, namely, thou shalt love thy neighbor as thyself. Love worketh no ill to his neighbor; therefore love is the fulfilling of the law." One of the joys of personal witnessing is to help a young Christian learn to say thanks by teaching him to pray, to emphasize that holy living is not by force, but by thankful response and willingness of heart. This becomes the beginning of a lifelong pilgrimage of changed living to the glory of God.

I close with this threefold summary.

First, use of the Bible is important, for God speaks through His Word. Memorize the location of key passages that will help you in your sharing of the good news. Use the Book of Romans.

Second, the good news of salvation in Jesus Christ is the only way of salvation. John 14:6: "I am the way, the truth, and the life, no man cometh unto the Father, but by me." The apostles said the same, "Neither is there salvation in any other, for there is none other name under heaven given among men, whereby we must be saved" (Acts 4:12). This makes it so urgent for us. Not only do we rejoice in the God of our salvation, but we know He is the only God, and Jesus is the only Savior. The burden and motivation to speak of Him in personal evangelism is the salvation of souls. We don't know whom God is pleased to save, thus we care about every soul that crosses our pathway, for it may be God's very purpose in placing that person there, that we direct him to the Savior.

Third, faith comes by hearing the Word of God (Rom. 10:17). The emphasis there is on the preached word. Personal witnessing is God's means to prepare the heart for that great work of salvation. None of us knows just when and how God saves a soul, but one thing is sure, He uses personal witnessing and preaching as the means to accomplish it. For that we must be eternally grateful to God.

It is His wonderful work.

# IV. Seeking the Salvation of the Lost

God is a God of order.

Within the covenant sphere He uses believing parents to nurture, influence, and mold the hearts of children. Outside the covenant sphere He uses believers to reach out to others to share the gospel with them and, by the work of His Holy Spirit, to draw them within the covenant sphere.

In mission work, God has bound together the preaching of the gospel and the personal witness of the believer as His ordained way to save souls. This is true in a mission field of labor and it is true in the established local church. The link between the local church and the non-Christian is the witness of the individual child of God.

True, mission outreach has as its focus the non-Christian. By saying this, we do not negate the care and burden we have for one who may already be converted but has not come to enjoy the true doctrine of the Bible or to enjoy the freedom of the new life in Christ that the Bible espouses. Both of these people become the burden of the missionary in his labors as well as of each one of us as we witness to our neighbors. There is something special about the unbeliever who is lost in sin and, without God's mercy to save him, will perish. Though the task may be more difficult, the urgency becomes more profound. Our heart of love reaches out to the most destitute because we know God is able to save, should He desire. When God desires this and brings it to pass, nothing can match the deep joy that flows from our hearts for His love and mercy shown to such a sinner. If you shed a tear of joy when your child makes public confession of faith, you can identify with what I am saying here. This converted heathen becomes your spiritual child in the Lord. Our admiration for God's sovereignty is renewed as we witness firsthand His power to save.

Now I want to focus on a simple question, what is the goal of personal evangelism?

The answer is, since personal evangelism is intimately connected with the preaching of the gospel, the goal is the same: the salvation of the sinner. To put it differently, the goal of personal evangelism is the conversion of the sinner to God. Now we have to explain that a bit, especially in light of so much confusion that takes place in connection with wrongful evangelism.

Frequently we hear that personal evangelism is "to win souls for Christ." I know the Bible uses that term in Proverbs 11:30, and when used from that perspective, it is proper. However, so much man-centered evangelism uses that term in connection with what is called "confrontational evangelism." The emphasis ends up this way: we witness to someone who is not a Christian and the goal is that, on the spot, at that very moment, the sinner is converted to God and becomes a Christian. The idea is that we must confront the sinner with the demands of the gospel and, if we do it correctly, this is the occasion for his immediate salvation. It is this sort of notion that has given rise to the notable "four spiritual laws," which supposedly have saved thousands of souls. We reject all such notions and do not see the role of personal evangelism that way. It is far more correct to speak of personal evangelism as "sowing seeds" and sharing the content of the Word of God with one who is interested and praying that the Holy Spirit will use it in His own time.

Similarly, we ought not to speak of the goal of personal evangelism as bringing in the masses for Sunday worship. Again, we believe that part of the blessing of God on personal evangelism is that God may use it to bring others under the preached word of God. But the man-centered emphasis of the modern "Church Growth" movement has the perspective that teams of members go out and witness to others and make the gospel so attractive that we may expect thousands to respond. This may produce a mega-church all right, but the focus is not on the pure word of the gospel, but rather on what man wants and finds attractive.

Still others speak of the Christian as being the "salt and light of the world." Their perspective on Matthew 5:13-16 is that the goal of personal evangelism is to get people to be a good element within society itself. Now, we would never deny that the Christian is the best citizen in the land and the best contributor for social responsibility, for that is true. But when we speak of the goal of evangelism on such a human, horizontal plane, we never come to grips with God's intended purpose in the salvation of His people.

Hence, we should be clear on the following goals as they relate to personal evangelism.

First, we must emphasize that, since the salvation of the human soul is God's domain and only He is able to accomplish it, we must set forth from the very outset that the one great goal of all evangelism, including personal evangelism as it relates to the preaching of the gospel, is the glory of our sovereign God. This is important because if we consciously include this in our *goal*, we will also be careful to incorporate in our methodology God-honoring methods. Nothing may detract from God's honor, and everything must contribute to it. The glory of God is the purpose of our entire existence, "That we should be to the praise of his glory who first trusted in Christ" (Eph. 1:12). Paul expresses it so beautifully in Romans 11:36: "For of him, and through him, and to him, are all things: to whom be glory forever. Amen." God has all the glory; we are called upon to acknowledge it by our praise.

Secondly, the Bible describes fallen man as being in a terrible condition of human depravity with its resultant state of guilt before God. As we begin to sow the seeds of the gospel in our personal evangelism, we do so with the humble prayer that God will begin to convict the sinner of his sins and of the need for forgiveness in the blood of Jesus. The darkness of human sin blinds the eyes and deceives the heart. Such sinners need to have the scales taken from their eyes and their hearts opened to the God of love. An honest dealing with sin is crucial for the appreciation of God's great gift in giving us His Son to be our Savior. The goal of all evangelism is the tears of the repentant sinner dried at the foot of the cross.

Thirdly, regarding those who are already saved and searching for a deeper faith, the goal of personal evangelism is to minister to such people and to share with them the knowledge we have of the Bible as it relates to both doctrine and life. Edifying the saints is an important aspect of evangelism, and every believer has the qualifications to minister to such fellow saints. Some may not understand the teachings of the Bible, or they may have backslidden and made a mess out of their lives. Yet, if they see in us something they desire for themselves, they are responding as Peter teaches us in I Peter 3:15: "But sanctify the Lord God in your hearts; and be ready always to give an answer to every man that asketh you a reason of the hope that is in you with meekness and fear." Meeting such needs is a glorious opportunity to share the gospel.

Finally, we ought to include one more aspect, and that is that the goal of personal evangelism is to lead people into the local church. This is often neglected today because so many "Christians" have been hurt by someone in the church or have convinced themselves they can be Christians without being part of a local church. This is wrong, and we must correct such notions. Hurt people must be encouraged to find healing and forgiveness within the body of Christ but also to learn that their perception of the church may be so ideal that it is far from reality. There is no perfect church; in fact, every church is far from perfection. Fellow sinners must learn to interact with each other in the way of loving, forgiving, and seeking strength to bear with one another's faults and burdens. The church is necessary for spiritual life. The Reformers correctly insisted, and this is expressed in our Reformed confessions, e.g., Belgic Confession, Article 28, that there is no salvation apart from the church of Jesus Christ. The church is our spiritual mother. Converts mentioned in the Bible were always added to the church (Acts 2:47).

In light of the goals mentioned above, we want to draw three conclusions. First, when we speak of the conversion of the sinner we include in that work of grace the conversion of the whole person. Salvation is the work of God that begins in the heart of man. Regeneration is the first work of God in the human heart, "except a man be born again, he cannot see the kingdom of God" (John 3:3). The heart is the center of man's spirituality, for "out of it are the issues of life" (Prov. 4:14). Jesus emphasized this as He taught, in distinction from the Pharisees, "For out of the heart proceed evil thoughts, murders, adulteries, fornications, thefts, false witness, blasphemies: these are the things which defile a man: but to eat with unwashen hands defileth not a man" (Matt. 15:19, 20). This is important. As we share the gospel with a non-Christian, we focus on his heart, and he must forsake all hatred and learn to love God and his neighbor.

It follows, then, that a changed heart will affect a man's entire nature. His mind will be affected, so that he thinks God's thoughts. His human will is also affected, so that his desires and affections are changed. He desires to please God and he enjoys God's fellowship more than the pleasures of sin. His emotions come under the power of God's transforming work. He learns to control his anger, he fears God rather than men, and such like. And, yes, even his body comes under the power of grace, for he knows that his body has now become the temple of God, which we have from God, and we are not our own but are bought with a price, in order that we may glorify God with our body and spirit which are God's (I Cor. 6:19, 20).

This change is not such that one no longer has to contend with sin in his nature. Rather, the work of salvation is God's work, which transcends the flesh. The old man of sin still remains, and the converted person has to learn to say yes to God and no to sin as he struggles to overcome the motions of sin in his flesh (Rom. 7:14ff.). The result of this spiritual tension is that his life is changed. Conversion results in a changed life. Almost all of Paul's epistles demonstrate this. The first part of each letter includes doctrinal teaching, which is followed by instruction on how a child of God serves God with his whole life.

Secondly, there is one important observation to be made in light of what we have just said. Such a conversion, which begins from the inside and affects the whole life of man, is the work of the Holy Spirit alone. No human being can convert a person from death to life. Ephesians 2, Ezekiel 37, as well as Acts 2 demonstrate that unsaved man is *dead* in sin. When we share the gospel in its early stages of personal evangelism, we know that there must be some powerful work of God if such a person is going to be saved. This is confirmed both by scriptural teaching and by personal experience. The dead sinner needs a work of grace administered by the Holy Spirit if conversion is to be realized. We never know if it is God's will to perform such a work in the individual with whom we may be sharing the gospel. We do know that God promises to bless our witnessing and to work by His Spirit in every soul it pleases Him to save. This gives us confidence and strength to press on.

Thirdly, since the Holy Spirit always works through the Word of God, the Bible, we must make extensive use of our Bibles when we speak to others. Human reasoning, quoting of great men, emotional appeals will not convert. The Holy Spirit works through the Word. Reading the Bible, explaining Bible passages, holding personal Bible Studies—all are used by God to set His truth before men. Again, this is what God promises. "All scripture is given by inspiration of God, and is profitable for doctrine, for reproof, for correction, for instruction in righteousness: that the man of God may be perfect, thoroughly furnished unto all good works" (II Tim. 3:16). Did not our Lord use this method when He contended with the devil? How could He shut the devil's mouth from telling lies? He thundered at him over and over, "It is written!" For those readers who have some experience in personal evangelism, you can testify from your own experience as well. It is amazing how you can speak abstractly or try to convince by human reason, and nothing seems to get through. Simply take your Bible, open it up to a number of passages that say what you wish to express, and the person responds, the light comes on, the Word convicts.

Finally, since the goal of evangelism is the conversion of the sinner, which only God is able to do, we must say in conclusion that such work requires diligent prayer. The New Testament is filled with references that emphasize the need to uphold preachers in prayer, e.g., Ephesians 6:18-20; Romans 15:30. Personal witnessing is not preaching, it is the preliminary work of God preparing one for preaching and therefore requires the same spiritual attention. Surely, in the work of ministering to the souls of lost people, the desire that God may do His work forces us to acknowledge how feeble and fallible are our efforts. At the same time, it is so assuring to look heavenward to behold by faith Jesus at the right hand of God, who sends His Spirit to accomplish what His soul desires to do.

As we recognize this, we confess that boasting about how many souls we saved is offensive both to God and to man. Rather, let him that glorieth, glory in the Lord.

# V. How to Practice Personal Evangelism

There are many passages of the Bible that shed light on the subject before us: how do I go about sharing the gospel with my neighbor? We will consider a few of them.

We first take a look at Luke 10:30-37. This is the well-known passage in which Jesus answers the question of the lawyer, "What shall I do to inherit eternal life?" Jesus posed another question, "What is written in the law?" The lawyer summarized it correctly: love God with all your heart, soul, strength, and mind and love your neighbor as yourself. This young man wanted to justify himself, so he continued, "Who is my neighbor?" In answer to this question, Jesus told the parable of the Good Samaritan. Obviously, the answer is that my neighbor is anyone whom God places upon my pathway who is in need. We act neighborly when we meet that need.

In the parable, it was the Samaritan who helped the wounded Jew, in distinction from the priest who passed by on the other side. The Samaritans were despised by the Jews, including this lawyer, but he was the one who acted neighborly in caring for the Jew by anointing his wounds and paying his expenses. By this, Jesus explained to the lawyer what the keeping of the law is all about. It is the act of loving the neighbor, any neighbor, by showing mercy to him in his hour of need. This may be a physical or a spiritual need.

The application for personal witnessing is obvious. What greater need does our neighbor have than salvation? The proof of our keeping the law of love is our personal witnessing to those who cross our pathway who are not Christians. We meet his needs by bringing the good news of salvation to him. We don't judge who he is. We don't put forth the effort because we think we will be successful. We simply meet his needs as we have opportunity when we encounter him on the pathway of life.

Paul's methodology of bringing the gospel, as recorded in I Thessalonians 1:7-12, is helpful. Since there is a close relationship between preaching the gospel and personal witnessing, we can learn from this passage. According to Acts 17, Paul persisted in bringing the gospel to the Thessalonians, even after he suffered persecution from many in the community. This opposition did not cause Paul to go "soft on the gospel." He tells us that he continued to bring the gospel, "not as pleasing men" (v. 4); "neither at any time used we flattering words, as ye know, nor a cloak of covetousness" (v. 5); "nor of men sought we glory" (v. 6). Paul did not change the message to make it less offensive when he dealt with this opposition. Notice what he says about the method or approach he used. "We were gentle among you, even as a nurse cherisheth her children" (v. 7). He was urgent and sincere: "Being affectionately desirous of you, we were willing to have imparted unto you, not the gospel of God only, but also our own souls, because ye were dear to us" (v. 8). More than anything, Paul confirmed the gospel with his own godly living, "Ye are witnesses, and God also, how holily and justly and unblamable we behaved ourselves among you that believe" (vv. 10-12).

Obviously, the first application of this passage is to the preaching of the gospel, whether on the mission field or in the established church. Yet, we can learn something from this passage for personal witnessing as well. We must be strongly convicted of the message of the gospel and never compromise it just to make it more acceptable to people. We must care for the souls of those with whom we share the gospel, even to the point of personal sacrifice. A harsh, confrontational, and judgmental approach only closes doors; we must also be gentle and sensitive to people's present beliefs or values. This applies particularly to our approach.

If they reject the gospel eventually, then we have to respond accordingly. Our walk and our talk must harmonize if we are to be effective.

One more passage is I Corinthians 9:19-23. In this letter to the Corinthians, Paul reminds them that he made himself servant to all. To the Jews, he became a Jew, to those without law as without law (being not without law to God, but under the law to Christ) that he might gain them that are without law. To the weak, he became as weak, to gain them. He said he was made all things to all men, that he might by all means save some. And this he did for the gospel's sake, that he might be partaker thereof with them. This is the classic passage that speaks especially of cross-cultural mission work. Paul, the great missionary, understood what it meant to be all things to all people without compromising the gospel. Sensitivity is evident in his writing this letter; he learned that from all his experiences.

The same things are important when we do personal evangelism with a non-Christian, who more than likely comes from a culture quite different from our own covenant life. We must take time to study his culture and religion, learn where we have similarities that might form bridges for conversation (as Paul did in Athens, Acts 17). Harshly judging him as wrong is not the right approach. Rather, we have to be as much like him as we can be without compromise. This is the challenge for all of us when we do personal evangelism. The goal is to "gain him" for Christ.

As we look more specifically at proper methodology, we can discard quickly a few wrong methods. We reject *Confrontational Evangelism*, or, as it is sometimes called, *Decisionism Evangelism*. This is the popular approach of those who hold to Arminian theology. It has come to expression in the "Four Spiritual Laws," which, we are told, if used properly can convert a person in a few minutes. The goal is to persuade people to accept Christ as their own

Savior. A person is assured of everlasting life by saying "yes" at the right moment. It is sealed by a brief prayer. Sadly, this builds egos for the people sharing the gospel and leaves the so-called convert deceived.

Another approach for personal evangelism is called *Accommodation Evangelism*. The goal here is to remove from the gospel message everything that might offend and include everything that makes it attractive. You are familiar with this approach in the mega-churches. Just come the way you are, get a cup of coffee, listen to some rock group, and perhaps listen to a well-trained entertainer who knows how to popularize Christian issues. On a more personal level, this is done by reducing the gospel to some comic book, by assuring people that there is truth in all religions, we just have to find the common ground among them. This approach is used by sports heroes who autograph baseballs on Sunday afternoon.

Then there is the *Salesmanship Evangelism*. The gospel is a product that is for sale, and you can use every form of advertising and salesmanship to persuade a person to become a Christian, just as you would to sell a used car. Slick ads, clever techniques, a Bible set forth in modern jargon, make up the components of the next sale, persuading people to buy into Christianity.

The Bible makes clear that God's method of saving souls is the *sowing of seeds*. Jesus sets this forth in Matthew 13:3-9 and 18-23 in the well-known parable of the sower. The Word of God, like seed, is sown and falls on different kinds of hearers. Paul uses the same language of sowing in 1st Corinthians 3:6-9: "I have planted, Apollos watered; but God gave the increase." The first application of this is to the preaching of the gospel. Under the preaching, the same method applies to personal witnessing. When we talk to others about the truth of God's Word and use God's Word in our evangelism, the Word of God is set forth, and as a seed it is sown in the hearts of the hearer according to God's will and purpose. This idea allows us to go slowly in our personal evangelism. Seeds sown take time to germinate and grow. We can begin sowing in the hearts of children. In God's own time it will bear fruit. We can use the help of others, books, literature, Bible study groups, and ultimately the Word preached itself.

From the perspective of sowing seeds, our personal evangelism can be done in two ways, by means of *Contact Evangelism* or by *Friendship Evangelism*. The difference between these two methods is the occasion for sharing. By contact evangelism we refer to the sudden, one-time opportunity that we have to be in the presence of another person whom God has caused to cross paths with us. How do we witness to such a person? By friendship evangelism we have the advantage of repeated opportunities of contact, and we can build upon them actually to establish a certain form of friendship that gives its own opportunities for sharing the gospel. Both of these methods are useful and under God's blessing will bear fruit in the heart and life of the person who receives the Word of God.

When we use *Contact Evangelism*, the points of contact vary a great deal. It may be as casual as standing in line for check-out at the shopping center. It might be at a business convention when you chat with someone over a cup of coffee. Opportunity can jump out at you when you distribute religious material in the neighborhood of your church. It might be when you are hospitalized and another person is in the same room as you are. You get the idea. These are momentary opportunities, when we can sow the seed of the Word of God in someone's life. You may never see the person again. Your pathways cross for this moment. Jesus calls you to be the Good Samaritan in the life of this person. Somehow you are alert and aware that there must be some opportunity to let this person know you are a Christian and that your faith makes a difference in your life and that you desire the same for him or her.

You can appreciate the concept of sowing seeds, for that is what you do. You sow a thought, an act of kindness, a word of encouragement, share some hope in what seems defeat. All these efforts speak loudly to people. You may never know what effect they had on them because you may never see them again. Yet, many people testify that they were influenced by just such a word from a Christian in such a casual moment.

What can we do in such a situation? Obviously, I have to be brief here, but let me give you something to ponder and, hopefully, to put into practice in your own way. Try to turn a conversation towards spiritual truth. This is most easy if you work at it and practice it. You can adore God for the beautiful weather in the presence of others. You can put a Christian perspective on the day's events, especially if it attracts attention. You can ask a person if he is a Christian, and take off from there. You can ask questions and gain knowledge, so that you can address a specific Christian truth that is very precious to you. It is very helpful to carry a tract that you can give to someone. The subject must deal with Christianity and the simple gospel message. You should be able to express in a few words why you are a Christian and that you have a burden for this person, if he demonstrates that he is not saved. You might inquire whether this person has any interest in learning the Christian faith, which is of course the Reformed faith. It is helpful to be able to recommend to him or her a book to read for further study, or you can always refer them to the Internet and your church's web page, which has loads of good material. You might exchange addresses for further contact. I still carry with me business cards, a habit I formed in Singapore, where everyone has them and exchanges them.

Then we also have *Friendship Evangelism*. Here we must exercise Christian caution, as friendship can quickly be used wrongfully. The idea here is to befriend someone whom you see often, with a view to getting closer to him and to influence his life in a Christian manner. This can be someone as close as a fellow member of the church who is struggling with some doctrine or practice of the church. Hopefully such a one is not an unbeliever, but rather a hurting Christian. It is always best to practice speaking about our faith to those who are closest to us on a daily basis. We speak about the gospel and its meaning and application within our Christian homes. We reach out to others in the church, and school setting. As we do this we feel comfortable talking about our faith and it becomes natural to do this with non-Christians who cross our pathway frequently. Think of your neighbor who lives next door to you. Think of your fellow worker on the job or fellow students in the university. Maybe you meet someone repeatedly in some sports situation, business meetings, clubhouse, social event, or whatever.

How can we reach out to such people and sow the seeds of the Word of God? It may be that you start out as we mentioned above. In this situation you have the advantage of follow up because you may be able to see each other again and build on past contact. The most important thing to keep in mind is that actions speak louder than words. This is critical because the more you see of each other the more you may see faults and bad habits and even sins. If we are going to sow the seeds of Scripture, we must put forth every effort that our life testifies we are Christians and that we walk the talk, as they say. This is the point of I Peter 3:15, 16, where we are exhorted to sanctify the Lord God in our hearts and be ready to explain to others the reason for our hope. Because the goal is repeated contact, we must engage in pleasant conversation. No one wants to talk repeatedly with a grouch or a pious critic who makes them feel uncomfortable. You have to prepare the soil by making yourself attractive as a Christian and projecting yourself in such a way that this person is envious of your life as a Christian. Our faith and practice is restrictive but liberating in a good

69

sense of the word. We must try to take an interest in the neighbor's life. We can do things together that allow us to interact, without compromising our faith. You figure it out; there are opportunities galore. The idea is that casual conversation may lead to more serious interest and hopefully to a more systematic discussion of some aspect of Christian faith and life. You must not rush this process, it may take years, but you are available and interested in the personal life of this neighbor.

Many converted Christians have mentioned that a one-on-one Bible Study was most helpful. When you have built up some trust in each other and some sort of friendship, you can suggest that the person come along to a Bible Study in the church or some public meeting that is a bit casual and not as formal as a worship service. Taking them along to church is the golden gate for which we all strive. Notice I didn't say invite them to church, but take them along. Make arrangements to sit with them and to help them through the service, as it is very difficult for someone to worship for the first time in his life. If this goes well, the person is ready for a pre-membership class taught by the pastor or elders.

Two things are important to emphasize in this connection. Teaching is the key to sowing seeds and making disciples. The Word of God is the textbook, and the Holy Spirit the author of life. We are the agents, and must humbly serve God in this capacity, praying with all diligence. Secondly, this is a process of learning and, like sowing seeds, there are no shortcuts. The seed needs moisture and warmth to germinate. It needs sunshine and rain to grow. And it takes a whole season to ripen and harvest. The seed of the Word is the same, and we must be like the Christian farmer who waits long and patiently for the harvest, which comes through the early and latter rain (James 5:7).

# VI. Equipping Ourselves for the Work

As we consider the subject of how we equip ourselves for the work of personal evangelism, I like to focus on five things.

First, *we must begin by checking our hearts.* Each one of us must ask himself this question, Am I right with my God? Personal evangelism, or personal witnessing, is a spiritual act that requires spirituality. All such spirituality is expressed by our own personal relationship with God in Jesus Christ.

Jesus makes this point in His Parable of the Lost Son, sometimes called the Parable of the Prodigal Son, recorded in Luke 15:11-32. We can quickly review the main points of this parable. The younger son requested the inheritance of his father before his father died, he received it, and he squandered it in a far country. He had a spiritual awakening there when things went very badly after he had wasted all his money. He recalled that the servants in his father's house had more comforts than he did. But he realized fully that he could not just pack up and return home. He had sinned against his father by placing greater value on his money than on his friendship with him in the home. Hence, he proposed to himself that the way of reconciliation involved two things. He had to admit to his father that his past action forfeited his claim to any benefits of being his son, since he had disowned his father. He had to tell his father that his request was not for recognition of sonship, but simply for a place in the paternal home as a servant. More than that, he had to admit that his past actions were sinful against his father and that he had to tell him, "I have sinned and am no more worthy to be called thy son" (v. 19).

Upon his return, this young man learned what paternal love was really like. His father was longing for his return, was glad to receive his son back, was ready to forgive him, and gave him a place of honor in the family. All of this was his expression of forgiveness in response to repentance. Obviously, this is the main point of the parable for all Christians.

When we are honest about our spiritual state and condition before God, we quickly identify with this prodigal. We know from our own experience our desperate state and our inability to do anything that makes us acceptable to our Father in heaven. We learn time and time again what love is really like—Father accepts us for the sake of Jesus His Son. Our acceptance is not based on our being good enough for Father, but rather in that Father makes us good enough for Himself in the death and resurrection of His own Son. Love flows from Father to us and is the source of our being accepted. The proof of our understanding such forgiveness is demonstrated by our love, which we return to Father and to Jesus His Son. We celebrate our acceptance by listening to our Father and feasting in His house. Our worship is our delight in Father. We marvel at the depth of His forgiveness and acceptance of such unworthy children.

By contrast, the elder brother, who was such a good fellow, goes into a rage. Even the father in the parable admits that the elder brother was a good young man. He did obey, he did keep the rules of the family, he did conform to all the desires and aspirations of the father. But he could not forgive his brother who had erred and gone astray. He criticized his father when he gave a feast for him. He poured out his criticism and judgment of his father and his brother. Why did he do this? The reason was that he did not know his own sins or unworthiness. He could see the faults of others but not his own. He was a Pharisee, self-righteous, judgmental, outwardly good but inwardly far from enjoying God's forgiving love.

What does this have to do with personal evangelism?

72

Everything. If we do not know our own personal sins and salvation in Jesus Christ, we act like the elder brother. So easily we can view ourselves as very good and acceptable to God. In the next breath we can so easily criticize others, our fellow church members, other Christians, our neighbors, and pat ourselves on the back and brag about how much more faithful we are. Such a spirit will never reach out to others, because it lacks the love that is necessary to do the work. The more self-righteous we are, the more judgmental we are of others. The next thing we do is to justify our refusal to share the gospel with unworthy sinners. A forgiven prodigal, such as we ought to be, is so appreciative of Father's love and acceptance that it motivates him to consider that what happened to him can by Father's mercy happen to the most unworthy of sinners who cross his path. Father may even use us as His instruments to lead others to the house of feasting, and nothing would make us more pleased with Father.

Second, to equip ourselves for personal evangelism *we need to understand that this activity is God's will for us and that our obedience to it is an answer to His call.* I put it this way deliberately. We must not think of personal witnessing as something that is extra and beyond the call of duty. Every Christian has the calling to be engaged in this activity. This is true because of his prophetic office, given to him by our Lord Jesus Christ. We have already spelled this out in detail, so here we just insert this point to keep this perspective. The call to serve King Jesus as a Christian includes three aspects: a prophetic, priestly, and kingly dimension. In connection with the prophetic aspect, we are anointed, by our union with Jesus Christ, to be able to speak His word to others. Parents do this in the instruction of their children; laborers do this when they describe the reason of the hope that is in them to fellow workers; we do this as neighbors in our interaction with them. The point that is important here is this, that we may properly compare the call of a pastor to the call of the Christian as prophet. They are different, surely, and must not be identified as one and the same. But we can say this, that just as important as the call from God to serve in the ministry is to the pastor, so important is the call to witness to every Christian. It is God's will that we do it. With the call is the promise of spiritual enabling. Since God calls us to engage in personal evangelism, we turn to Him for wisdom and strength to do it. The call helps us to see the seriousness of the labor and the strengthening that comes from the God who called us.

Third, *we must examine our motives for doing this work of personal evangelism.* We can look at this from different points of view.

If we are *not* engaged in this activity, we might ask ourselves why this is. There are a number of possibilities. Does it seem to you, perhaps, that the church emphasizes the *preaching* of the gospel to such an extent that the importance of your prophetic role as a believer is minimized? I am convinced that the PR position regarding the official preaching of the gospel does not do this. If you do not busy yourself with personal evangelism, might it, instead, be due to spiritual coldness as mentioned above? Or might there be some sin in your life that you would have to abandon if you are to get sincere about your personal witnessing? If you have any sin that controls you or that you commit, obviously you would have to abandon that sin if you will give a good testimony. Examples of this would be cursing, drunkenness, filthy conversation, or what have you. Do you want to convince yourself that you don't have to witness to others—in order that you can hide your own sin in your bosom? Another possibility is that you may feel completely inadequate and overwhelmed by this activity and convince yourself that you are just not cut out for it. None of the above is an adequate reason for our not practicing personal evangelism.

74

It is also possible that we may practice personal evangelism but from *wrong motives*. We might say, I need more fulfillment in my life as a Christian, and if I witness to others, it gives me this dimension. Now it is true that this does result from practicing evangelism, but we must be very careful that our doing it is not pride or self-serving. We can add to this that some Christians might view witnessing for Christ and God as an act of good that helps them gain favor with God and acceptance by Him. Then we have a wrong idea of faith and works. Our acceptance by God is not based on anything we do. It is based on the perfect sacrifice of Christ on the cross and His perfect obedience in keeping the law of righteousness for us. We might imagine that if we witness to others, we serve our fellow man in the best way. Again, that is true, but our motive for serving our God must never be *man*. It must always be *God*. For God's sake we must reach out and share the gospel with others, that it may please God to use us to introduce a non-Christian to God and His Son. We must not do it to please the church. Yes, it pleases the church when members exercise their living faith and witness, but the motivation must not be to please men, not even our pastor or elders. It must always be to please God and His Son, Jesus Christ.

Thus we can summarize the proper motivation. This involves three things. 1.) It is in obedience to God who has called us to this prophetic office and equips us to exercise it to His glory. The chief motive of all mission work, and personal witness as well, is to bring glory to our God. We do this when we faithfully speak His word of truth to all who ask us a reason of the hope within. 2.) We do it out of love for our neighbor for God's sake. Again, it is not simply love for our neighbor as a human being. It is that of course, but we must love him for God's sake. God placed this neighbor upon our pathway. This may have the express purpose that, as we demonstrate God's love for us and we show that to him, he comes to know the Father as the prodigal son of the parable. 3.) Personal evangelism adds a beautiful dimension to our personal life as a Christian. We are blessed by this activity, and God tells us this as well. We are enriched spiritually when we see a non-Christian struggle through his doubts and fears, his stubbornness and sins, and come to the cross of Jesus for forgiveness and to the family of God for friendship. Members are personally enriched as the entire congregation is blessed through the wonder of grace God works in their midst.

Fourth, *we must take inventory of the gifts God has given to us for this work.* We have emphasized repeatedly that the call to faithful witness includes the assurance of divine enabling. Even though it is true that God can use a nominal Christian to bring this word of witness, as He sometimes does in the pulpit of the church as well, it is not God's usual way, and we do not want to rely on such abstraction. Evidence of the divine call is associated with the giving of the gifts.

Hence, as we consider the subject of equipping ourselves for this notable activity of personal evangelism, we must examine ourselves regarding gifts for this work. We carefully distinguish these gifts from the temporary gifts of the Spirit given to the apostles in the early church, such as miracles and speaking in tongues, which have ceased (I Cor. 13:8). God also gives special gifts to those who are called to the holy office of ministers, elders, and deacons. We are speaking of the gifts given to fulfill the prophetic office of every believer. Actually, they are no different than those given to the special offices, except that they pertain to the office of believer. The description of these gifts in I Timothy 3 and Titus 1, as they relate to the special offices, can certainly apply to every believer. The point is that not every believer has received these gifts, and therefore they do become the measure of those called to the special offices, in whom these gifts must be present. Every believer who possesses these gifts (and there are certainly more believers

that possess these gifts than those who serve in special
office) is blessed by God to use them in personal evangelism.
This is the answer to women who impose themselves on the
office of minister of the gospel, claiming they have the gifts.
Having the gifts does not determine the call to holy office,
which is restricted by Scripture to men only. These women
must be encouraged to use such gifts in serving God in
other ways, both in the church and in the world. To some
degree every Christian has these gifts, but some possess
them in a greater measure. And by grace these gifts can
also be cultivated for greater service. If you feel yourself
inadequate or unqualified to engage in personal evangelism, do not use this as an excuse to abandon your calling.
Rather, search carefully your spiritual condition before God
and sort out where you lack and what needs development,
and then focus on that. Paul said in I Timothy 4:7 that we
must exercise ourselves unto godliness. The word there is
the same as a gymnast, which indicates persistence, repeti-
tive practice to perfect the skills.

Fifth, *we must remind ourselves that our preparation for
evangelism includes the use of prayer.*

As is true in all areas of spiritual conduct, such work is
not natural, it is a wonder of grace. This is the answer to
any lack of incentive or ability to do it. Lack of incentive is
natural because it is the response of the natural man to
God's wonderful work of grace. We must never "give in" to
such thoughts and responses. As Christians we are no
longer under the control of our natural man. If we were,
then we could rightly say, "I can't, and therefore I won't
practice personal evangelism." Rather, the perspective of
the inspired apostle Paul encourages us to express, after
our struggle with our personal demons, "I thank God
through Jesus Christ our Lord that I am delivered from the
body of this death so that I can serve Him with my sanctified mind and soul."

The only way we can get out of the prison of our own weaknesses, and even our sins, is through the grace of God in Jesus Christ. These blessings of anointing, which are so important for us in order to fulfill our holy prophetic office, come to us through fervent prayer. When we ask God for the presence of His Holy Spirit, He provides this for us through worship on the Lord's Day and as we engage in daily family and personal prayer and worship. Spiritual stamina, which is essential for difficult and challenging work, comes to us from our heavenly Father as He administers it to us through Jesus Christ our Lord. We must never measure our ability without taking into account what God is able to do as He equips us.

These five areas of consideration are important for us as we prayerfully equip ourselves for this great work that God assigns to us.

# VII. Personal Evangelism's Impact on Church Extension

With this chapter we bring to a close our consideration of the work of evangelism in the established church. As we noted before, most of this work is done by a local church extension committee. This committee is instructed to come up with projects and ideas for extending the gospel beyond the confines of the local congregation. The focal point of congregational involvement is the worship services. The pastor, elders, and deacons, along with all the members, lift up their testimony of praise to Jehovah in the midst of the neighborhood. This act alone is most significant as a form of witness or evangelism to the world. Usually we put a signboard on the lawn in front of the church to announce our worship services, and add, "Visitors Welcome." Yet, we all know that seldom, if ever, does a non-member come to worship with us because of that signboard. We are sincere in our invitation, but it is quite ineffective in moving people to come inside. Some churches make it more "attention getting" by using the electronic format with catchy sayings. One wonders whether such gimmicks are not more distractions than actually aids in evangelism.

Non-members must be invited to come and worship. This being true, our church extension committees are given the mandate to come up with programs that go beyond our worship services to acquaint people with our ministry as a church and to invite them to participate with us in the good news of the gospel.

In this book we have tried to demonstrate that all these efforts by the church extension committee must involve personal evangelism by our membership if they are to attain the goal. The key to any effective outreach effort must include our members consciously and actively reaching out to neighbors and acquainting them with our efforts and inviting them to participate.

In this chapter I want to demonstrate this more specifically.

When we assess various possibilities of outreach projects, we quickly realize that some efforts must be rejected because of their secular emphasis. I have in mind the efforts of a church to be a community church and establish some sort of contact with neighbors by hosting an antique auto show in the parking lot. This might draw a crowd of auto enthusiasts, but more than likely if any effort is put forth to add a religious flavor, it would be offensive because people would then readily know that the auto show was a ruse for religious promotion.

There may be times when a society of the church or school may sponsor a public event such as a soup supper, a pancake breakfast, or such like in which the extended families and people of the community are invited. This is usually done for goodwill, especially in small communities. Even then, with some planning such as adding the singing of a vocal group of the church or a brief message by the pastor, it is possible to use such opportunities for evangelism.

I know instances where a neighborhood meal was promoted in connection with some event that easily has religious overtones. Thanksgiving Day, Christmas, Mother's Day, or something of that sort can provide an opportunity to invite the neighbors to visit the church for some eating and fellowship that includes religious music and a message. Social and spiritual can coincide rather easily in such instances.

It ought to be obvious that if we avoid secular events completely and focus on those that include an opportunity to have spiritual fellowship with the neighbors of the church, such events can contribute to significant outreach. Personal evangelism comes to the foreground in two ways. First, the members must invite the people to come to the event; this is the most effective way to have people come. Second, the members must interact with these neighbors once they show up and demonstrate a loving and caring interest in their lives and well-being. These events blossom when the members exercise their calling to share the gospel by personal evangelism.

Let me now list some possible events and activities that church extension committees could consider. The purpose of this list is to demonstrate that *all* of the activities prosper when the members engage in personal evangelism in connection with the event.

We hold public meetings, whether our worship services, public lectures, Bible Studies, or Vacation Bible School. Obviously, we do not equate public worship with the other ways of teaching. Our emphasis here is simply that they are public and we desire others to come and attend. The worship service is the intimate fellowship between Christ and His church, to be sure. The preaching is Christ speaking to His beloved to whom the church responds in affectionate words of praise. Even then, we desire visitors—we desire Christ to add to this church such as should be saved. Hence we seek the presence of visitors and inquirers at our worship service.

From this point of view, the same is true with public lectures, when a specific topic is considered for the benefit of the listeners. You may have discussed a topic over coffee with your neighbor, and now your pastor is going to give a lecture on the same subject. You will be excited to invite this neighbor to come and listen. Be sure you offer to pick him up or meet him at the door and sit with him, as this helps greatly to overcome the barrier of unfamiliar surroundings.

By Bible Studies we refer to those sponsored by the local congregation and held in the church building, to which visitors are always welcome. In addition, we also can have specially conducted Bible Studies in other areas of the community. These can be advertised and promoted in the community. The purpose of such studies is to have non-members come to learn the Christian perspective, or more specifically the Reformed faith.

The same is true for Vacation Bible School. It is directed to neighborhood children. Care must be taken that the effort to organize a VBS is not simply a baby-sitting service for neighborhood moms or a fun-time for kids with little or no religious meaning. When planned correctly, VBS can be effective to reach children with the gospel. It is a time when covenant moms can share their skills of teaching (their prophetic office) with children of the neighborhood as well as their own. It ought to be clear that the success of VBS is contingent on the membership acquainting people with the meetings and inviting them to come. These may be neighbors, colleagues at work, fellow students at school, extended family, or such like. The point is that we have been talking to these people about our faith regularly, we have shared with them many concerns, which include the value of children. They know the burden of our heart, and now there will be an opportunity for them to send their children to a VBS where such truths are taught and cherished.

We can make great use of audio and video recordings of our public meetings when extended promotion is given by our members who talk about Sunday's sermons and public lectures and then offer copies to neighbors or fellow workers. We can hold seminars or workshops on subjects such as child-rearing, marriage, evangelism. Much work goes into preparing these messages, and with a little effort the recordings of these messages can be very useful for promoting the truth as it relates to these areas of doctrine and life. Here too, the efforts of a church extension committee are limited to advertising in some appropriate manner. It is far more effective if everyone who has attended or who has enjoyed the tapes of such meetings puts forth effort to talk about them with others and distribute them far and wide. We wonder how we can have opportunity to witness? Here is just such an opportunity. This is the key role of personal evangelism.

We face the same problem with our literature. A good place to start is to sit down with our people and ask them what sort of subjects and questions they encounter when they talk spiritually with their neighbors. Notice, I did not say what kind of subject do *we* want to talk about with our neighbor. I ask, rather, what sort of subject do *they*, the neighbors, want to talk about. We will discover that concerning most of those subjects we do not have an appropriate pamphlet or tract that we can give to them. This exercise will help us focus on the needs and interests of our neighbors so that we can converse with them. It will also help prompt us to write pamphlets and tracts that address these subjects. You notice that if we do this sort of thing, once again the key force is not the production of the pamphlet, but the need for and distribution of this material. That involves personal evangelism.

There are many other activities that evangelism committees can consider.

In our efforts for mass distribution of material, we must exercise care that we do it legally. We must keep in mind that we live in a world where many people are offended by efforts for outreach, and it may even be prohibited by law. This may relate to street evangelism, which is forbidden in some areas, or it may be illegal to go from house to house, which is called solicitation, and public signs are posted warning against such activity. We must exercise care not to violate such laws, even though we may have the best of intentions to evangelize.

There are, however, many places and ways in which public distribution of materials is permitted. This may be anything from having a booth at the county fair, to going from door to door in neighborhoods. It can include hospital visitation, prison ministry, spending time with old folks in a rest home. In many of these instances there are certain restrictions listed, or at least there is a certain behavior that becomes a Christian, and we ought to learn good manners and sensitivities in those areas where we are allowed to evangelize. But the point I want to make here is that all these efforts involve personal evangelism in which the individual Christian is empowered by the Holy Spirit, who enables him to fulfill his prophetic office as given by Christ.

Some of our evangelism committees spend a lot of time and effort in newspaper evangelism. This is hard work for the writer of such articles. It takes a certain skill to set forth the truth of God's Word as it relates to a specific topic and to say it in a way that today's world can understand. One of the biggest obstacles we have to evangelism is the language we use. We have beautiful theological words that precisely identify truth. They are of utmost importance to us who are within the household of faith. It enables us to preach and communicate effectively together. Yet, we must be aware that when we evangelize those who are not famil-iar with the Bible and the historic truths, we have to use language that is understandable to the general public. This is why it is so difficult. Now, after all this work is expended in producing such a public testimony of truth, unless all of us consider it our duty to promote such writing, it will pass virtually unnoticed. What a splendid idea to cut out the writing and take it along to work and point it out to those who are around you. Did they notice this writing in the paper? What do they think of it? Do they agree and, if not, why not? Then personal evangelism contributes to the effectiveness of the efforts of the evangelism committee.

I want to close with one area of outreach that is most up-to-date and also very effective. That is the world-wide-web of the Internet. Our denomination has put out a very thorough web page through the efforts of Rev. VanBaren. Many of our individual churches are doing the same. I am sure that, as time goes on, we will learn many new ways to be more effective. As technology works its way down to the common folk, we will all learn how to make greater use of the posted sermons, messages, and information that abounds. Once again, what are you doing as a reader to promote the web? Yes, one thing about the Internet is that anyone can run a search program and discover any of our literature on the net. A personal touch, however, is the real key for promoting the gospel of the Reformed faith. Our denominational web page address (www.prca.org) is so easy that anyone can remember it and can refer people to it. So often you may not have a pamphlet handy, or you know there is a recording of a certain speech or sermon, and you wish you had it with you to give to the person to whom you are speaking. Just remember, almost all this material is available to anyone who has access to the web—and that is almost everyone. All you need to do is refer them to the denominational web page. Make use of it in your personal evangelism. It is a powerful tool that God has provided for us.

I trust that this book may motivate you, the reader, to take seriously your own role in personal evangelism and to come to appreciate that you too can make a contribution to the good work that your church extension committee is putting forth. As we promote their efforts, we will have plenty of opportunity to explain the truth as it is in Christ Jesus.

We close with a reminder that personal evangelism is God's work through us. We must be obedient to Him and pray that His Holy Spirit will use us to promote the gospel to His glory.

Printed in the United States
200619BV00002B/313-1023/A